IMAGES OF WAR

THE RUSSIAN ARMY
IN THE
FIRST WORLD WAR

Officers of the 17th *Arkhangelogorodsky* Infantry Regiment.

IMAGES OF WAR

THE RUSSIAN ARMY IN THE FIRST WORLD WAR

RARE PHOTOGRAPHS FROM WARTIME ARCHIVES

Nik Cornish

Pen & Sword
MILITARY

First published in Great Britain in 2014 by
PEN & SWORD MILITARY
an imprint of
Pen & Sword Books Ltd,
47 Church Street,
Barnsley,
South Yorkshire
S70 2AS

ISBN 978 184884 752 1

The right of Nik Cornish to be identified as Author of this Work has been asserted by him in accordance with the Copyright, Designs and Patents Act 1988.

A CIP record for this book is available from the British Library.

Typeset by CHIC GRAPHICS

Printed and bound by CPI Group (UK) Ltd, Croydon, CR0 4YY

Pen & Sword Books Ltd incorporates the imprints of Pen & Sword Archaeology, Atlas, Aviation, Battleground, Discovery, Family History, History, Maritime, Military, Naval, Politics, Railways, Select, Social History, Transport, True Crime, and Claymore Press, Frontline Books, Leo Cooper, Praetorian Press, Remember When, Seaforth Publishing and Wharncliffe.

For a complete list of Pen & Sword titles please contact
Pen & Sword Books Limited
47 Church Street, Barnsley, South Yorkshire, S70 2AS, England
E-mail: enquiries@pen-and-sword.co.uk
Website: www.pen-and-sword.co.uk

Contents

Acknowledgements and Photograph Credits

This book is dedicated to my mum, my partner Angie, my children Alex, Charlotte and James and all those service personnel of the Russian armed forces who fought and died during the First World War in what W.S. Churchill so rightly called the Forgotten War – the Eastern Front, 1914–18.

I should like to extend my sincere gratitude to the following chums who gave so kindly of their support and time during the writing of this book: Norbert Hofer, Dmitry Belanovsky, Stephen Perry and Andrei Simonov – thanks lads!

Images are taken from the following sources:

Courtesy of the Central Museum of the Armed Forces, Moscow via www.stavka.org.uk: p. 15 T, p. 25 B, p. 26 all, p. 27 T, p. 28 T, p. 39 all, p. 41 all, p. 50 T, p. 77, p. 78 T , p. 81 B, p. 82 all, p. 84 B, p. 85 B, p. 92 T, p. 93 T, p. 94 B, p. 95 B, p. 97 all, p. 98 B, p .111 B, p. 113 T, p. 120 B, p. 121 all, p. 122 T, p. 123 all, p. 125 T, p. 129 T, p. 136 T, p. 139 T, p. 140 T.

From the fonds of the RGAKFD, Krasnogorsk via www.stavka.org.uk: p. 13 B, p. 24 B, p. 35 all, p. 57 B, p. 78 B, p. 80 T, p. 83 T, p. 85 T, p. 96 B, p. 99 T, p. 105 B, p. 108 B, p. 109 all, p. 110 all, p. 111 T, p. 113 B, p. 120 T, p. 125 B, p. 126 T.

From Nik Cornish at www.stavka.org.uk: p. 13 T, p. 14 all, p. 15 B, p. 21, p. 22 all, p. 23 all, p. 25 T, p. 28 B, p. 29 all, p. 30 all, p. 36 all, p. 37 all, p. 38 all, p. 40 all, p. 41 all, p. 42 all, p. 43 all, p. 48 all, p. 49 all, p. 50 B, p. 51 all, p. 52 all, p. 53 all, p. 54 all, p. 55 all, p. 56 all, p. 57 T, p. 63, p. 64 all, p. 65 all, p. 66 all, p. 67 all, p. 68 all, p. 69, p. 70 all, p. 71 all, p. 72 all, p. 79 all, p. 80 B, p. 81 T, p. 83 B, p. 84 T, p. 86 all, p. 92 B, p. 93 B, p. 94 T, p. 95 T, p. 96 T, p. 98 T, p. 99 B, p. 100 B, p. 106 all, p. 107, p. 108 T, p. 112 all, p. 114 all, p. 122 B, p. 124 all, p. 126 B, p. 127 all, p. 128 all, p. 129 B, p. 130 B, p. 136 B, p. 137 all, p. 138 all, p. 139 B, p. 140 B, p. 141 all, p. 142 all, p. 143 all, p. 144 all.

Courtesy of S.J. Perry: p. 24 T, p. 27 B, p. 100 T, p. 104, p. 105 T.

Preface

The concept that underpins this book is simply to provide the general reader of military history with a heavily illustrated overview of the First World War from a Russian perspective.

I hope that this book goes some way to de-mystifying the operations in that theatre and sheds light on events other than the Battle of Tannenberg, the cataclysmic events of the Russian Revolutions of 1917 and the subsequent horror of the Russian Civil War. Furthermore, some readers may be encouraged to a deeper study of this neglected backwater of the First World War – indeed, it will certainly reward those with an interest in the exotic.

The Russian army fought on two fronts against three empires, Germany, Austria-Hungary and Turkey, all of which fielded not inconsiderable armies. It also dealt with a major internal uprising towards the middle of 1916 when the non-Russian population of Turkestan rose up against the Tsar in protest against the introduction of conscription.

During the last twenty years or so it has become much easier to access sources in the former Soviet Union, indeed, with political constraints removed, the study of the First World War and the Russian contribution to the Allied cause have become acceptable, even popular, in Russian academic circles. If this book helps to generate Western efforts in this direction, then it will have succeeded in achieving one of my aims.

For the sake of comparison with events on other fronts I have used the Gregorian calendar thus avoiding the irritation of adding thirteen days to Russian dates. The Gregorian replaced the Julian calendar under the Soviet regime in February 1918. I apologise to purists as many, more academic, books tend to use the Julian system until February 1918 whereas the majority of memoirs use the older dating style. Austria-Hungary is referred to as Austria and its Chief-of-Staff as von Hotzendorf not Conrad, as is quite often the case.

The images used throughout are, with few exceptions, drawn from archives in Russia and the states of the former USSR.

Introduction

For generations the Russian armies that marched to war during the summer of 1914 have suffered from the popular Western perception that they were ill-prepared, poorly led sheep marked for slaughter at the hands of the Kaiser's superbly officered, well-equipped troops while the Tsar and his family occupied their time with mysticism and domesticity. However, this view of the Russian army is somewhat at odds with the reality.

During the course of the preceding century Russia's military record had been an interesting one. Having contributed significantly to the defeat of Napoleon's armies between 1812 and 1814, her strategic objectives re-focused on the dismemberment of the Ottoman Turkish Empire via the Caucasus and the Balkans and expansion into central and eastern Asia from bases in Siberia. The latter campaigns had no significant impact on Russia's theory of war or the composition of her armies. However, the three wars fought against the Turks, 1828–9, the Crimean War 1854–5 and the Russo-Turkish War of 1877–8 did leave their mark, particularly the latter as it led to the beginnings of military modernisation with the introduction of a new field gun, infantry rifle and machine gun. Furthermore, it highlighted the weakness of the army's supply network and lack of medical facilities. Unfortunately, it also decided for many European military theorists that any subsequent wars would be short.

Russia's next war was with the coming power in Asia – Japan. By this time, 1904, the new rifle and artillery piece had been issued in large numbers, as had several dozen machine guns of different types. During this conflict the war revolved around two points. First, a significant part of the Japanese army in Manchuria was tied down besieging the Russian naval base at Port Arthur. Secondly, the majority of the Japanese troops were attempting to bring the Russians to battle. The war of movement ended with a series of engagements known collectively as the Battle of Mukden which was fought between 20 February and 10 March 1905. The Japanese plan was to outflank the Russians from the west, hold in the centre and to the east, then trap them in a double encirclement. As this plan unfolded the Russian commander and Minister of War, General A.N. Kuropatkin, responded indecisively and ineffectively. Attempting to control over 300,000 men spread along a front of 120km proved almost impossible. The field telephone system often broke down or their diaphragms froze and communications officers fell back on mounted couriers and runners. As a result of this problem and the lack of any roads not churned to mud by the thaw, it proved difficult to move reserves with any speed. Furthermore, the fall of Port Arthur, at the cost of 60,000 Japanese casualties over the four months of the siege, had released Japanese reinforcements and Kuropatkin ordered his men to withdraw before they were encircled.

The destruction of Russia's Baltic Sea Fleet at the Battle of Tsushima in May 1905 and increasing domestic problems left Tsar Nicholas II no alternative but to accept the terms of the Treaty of Portsmouth (USA) in September 1905 and end the war.

Internal upheavals led to the military being deployed in an internal security role across the length and breadth of the empire. Nor were the armed forces themselves immune to disorder, a Guards regiment mutinied briefly and there were several instances of troops refusing to fire on demonstrators. But these events were small beer when compared with the activities of the crew of the *Potemkin*, a battleship of the Black Sea Fleet. Having mutinied but failing to gain much support from the fleet, the *Potemkin*'s crew sailed from Sevastopol, in late June 1905, to Odessa, cruising the Black Sea until scuttling their ship in Constanza harbour and surrendering to the Romanian authorities some ten days later.

By 1907 the revolutionaries were either in prison, in exile or in hiding and Tsar Nicholas II had restored order by a mixture of repression and reform. Although a parliament – the Duma – had been created, the Tsar still retained much of his autocratic, decision-making power, including the right to dissolve the Duma. Russia's return to tranquillity was paralleled by an upsurge in economic activity, increased government revenue and the consequent expansion of the military budget. The latter was overseen by General V.A. Sukhomlinov who was appointed Minister of War in 1909. Sukhomlinov set about lobbying for an expansion of the armed forces which began in 1910 and continued with a series of small projects that culminated in the acceptance by the Tsar of the Great Programme in late 1913. Under the terms of the Great Programme the army would grow by over 500,000 infantry, the artillery to more than 8,000 guns and the Military Air Fleet would expand significantly. The timeline for this project ended, ominously with hindsight, in 1917. The Duma gave its approval on 22 June 1914 less than one week before the assassination of the Archduke Franz Ferdinand would generate the crisis that plunged Europe into the First World War. Nevertheless, Russia's leaders were not pessimistic: they felt they were as prepared for a short war as any other belligerent.

The popular Western image of Russia's army before the war was one of large numbers of men prepared to fight and die unquestioningly for the Tsar against external or internal enemies. By 1914 the Russians were readying themselves to field a more professional, modern army than many expected.

Tsar Nicholas II, seen here reviewing the *Konvoi* (Personal bodyguard) during 1916, believed in a mystical bond linking the royal family and the armed forces. His own military career was limited to service in the Guard Hussars before his accession to the throne in November 1894 at the age of 26. His 12-year-old son and heir the Tsarevich Alexei is seen by his side.

Part of the Great Programme was the upgrading of the artillery. Here a group of officer cadets undergo training with a Schneider 122mm howitzer. This French import was later built under licence in Russia. It fired a 23kg shell up to almost 8,000m.

As in every conflict it was the poor bloody infantry that would shoulder the worst of things in the front line. However, no amount of training could prepare the men for what was to come. Here a Russian infantry unit supports artillery. The gun is a 76mm M1902 piece. Domestically designed and built by the Putilov Company, it was the standard field gun throughout the period and could fire up to twelve rounds per minute.

These three Don Cossack cavalrymen were part of the vast cavalry arm that the Russians maintained. The Don Host provided some fifty-four regiments on notification of mobilisation. Each of the hosts was identifiable by the colour of the stripe down their breeches, in this case it was red.

News of Germany's declaration of war was greeted, certainly in the urban areas, with patriotic demonstrations. However, as one politician commented in the countryside, 'eternal silence reigned'. It was the peasantry who would bear the lion's share of conscription and casualities. St Petersburg, where these troops march to their muster point, was renamed the less Germanic Petrograd in late August 1914.

Chapter One

Where Shall We Fight?

At 1800hr on 31 July 1914 Tsar Nicholas II issued the order for the general mobilisation of his empire's armed forces. At midnight that night Germany declared war on Russia. Now the moment had come to test Sukhomlinov's declaration that, 'Russia is ready'. Men travelled to their assembly points filling the ranks of the thirty-seven army corps that made up the standing army and swelling the numbers in another thirty-five reserve divisions while a further seven infantry divisions were called up from the lower reserve categories.

The infantry was divided into an army corps each of guards and grenadiers, twenty-five line corps and three corps, two corps and five corps that comprised the Caucasian, Turkestan and Siberian armies respectively. These armies were stationed in and responsible for the security of those regions but would provide reinforcements for other theatres if required. A first-line infantry army corps was made up of 2 divisions each comprising 4 4-battalion regiments, with a battalion numbering roughly 1,000 men of all ranks. Corps troops included a battalion of sappers, 2 field artillery brigades of 6, 8 gun batteries and a *divizion* (half regiment) of 2 6-gun light howitzer batteries. In 1914 every first line regiment included a *kommando* (unit), of eight machine guns, a communications detachment and sixty-four specially trained scouts. A varying number of corps were allocated to the armies which would operate in groups known as 'fronts' under the Supreme Commander-in-Chief's HQ known as the Stavka. The reserve divisions, numbered 53rd to 84th, were organised in the same manner but included less modern artillery. Conscription across the twelve military districts of the empire began at 21, however; Moslems, Finns and Buddhists were exempted but allowed to enrol as volunteers.

With the largest number of mounted troops in the world the Russian army mobilised twenty-four cavalry and Cossack divisions. Each comprised 4 regiments of approximately 900 officers and men per regiment. A detachment of eight machine guns, a *divizion* of two, six-gun, horse artillery batteries, along with scouts, communications and demolition sections completed the establishment of a cavalry division. Although the terms hussar, dragoon and lancer were still in use, they were purely honorific. When fully mobilised the army would grow from 1.4 to nearly 5 million – the Russian steamroller of popular European legend.

However, it was not so much the army itself as what to prioritise that placed Russia's strategists in a quandary in the years leading up to 1914. The mobilisation and deployment planning of the pre-war years had been fraught with discussion and debate. Throughout the nineteenth century Russian planning had assumed an initial period of defensive operations while the army mobilised from the depths of the interior. To this end a group of fortified areas had been built to cover the major road and rail junctions and river crossing points. These fortifications would hold up the advance of enemies identified as Austria-Hungary, Germany and probably Romania operating together as Russia's armies gathered.

However, during the decade before 1914 this defensive mentality had been challenged by those who preferred a more offensive approach. The result was a series of compromises which left many senior officers at loggerheads with one another. The major fortified areas were in Russian Poland and western Ukraine, sited to hold up an invasion aimed at St Petersburg, Moscow and possibly Kiev and it was decided to retain and upgrade these following the success of the Port Arthur defences against Japan. The western part of Russian Poland, which formed a salient with Germany to the north and west and Austria-Hungary to the south, was to remain undefended and its infrastructure undeveloped. However, the speeding up of mobilisation, as a result of improvements in the railway network from the interior, had led to an agreement with Russia's ally France to launch an invasion of Germany's East Prussian province less than three weeks after mobilisation began. But there were those Russian officers who felt that it was Austria-Hungary that posed the more immediate threat and that an invasion of Austria's province of Galicia would be a more profitable use of resources. As well as the dismemberment of Turkey, Russia also anticipated the collapse of the Hapsburg Empire and the subsequent scramble for territory and coveted the province of Galicia. Consequently, plans were drawn up that led to the weighting of forces assigned to fight against Germany and Austria that were variable depending upon the threat posed by each. In the event of war two fronts would be created, the South-Western (SW) to invade Austria-Hungary and the North-Western (NW) to invade East Prussia. Under the instructions a period of grace was allowed for mobilisation, depending on where corps would be assigned as the nature of the threat revealed itself.

The likelihood of war with Turkey was factored in and the Army of the Caucasus as well as the Black Sea Fleet was in the process of being increased under the terms of the Great Programme as the occupation of Constantinople and the absorption of eastern Anatolia were both long-term Russian aims. Indeed, planning for a seaborne assault on Constantinople had been underway for some time. But as Russia was not at war with Turkey during August 1914 troops were sent from the Caucasus to bolster the Austro-German fronts when war was declared.

The Russian army marched off to war under the terms of Plan 19 variant A (revised) which committed thirty-four infantry divisions to the invasion of Austria and twenty-nine infantry divisions to the invasion of East Prussia.

The armies of SW Front deployed in an arc that curved around the Austrian border from Ivangorod to the Romanian border, respectively Fourth, Fifth, Third and Eighth armies under the command of General N.I. Ivanov along a front roughly 350km long. The gaps between the armies were to be covered by men of the fourteen cavalry divisions. The plan was for Fourth and Fifth armies to advance against the Austrian left as they moved eastwards to invade Russia. Eighth and Third armies were to advance westwards towards Lemberg, the capital of Austrian Galicia.

NW Front consisting of the twenty-nine infantry divisions of First and Second armies was under the leadership of General I.G. Zhilinski. NW Front was tasked with invading East Prussia from the south with Second Army and from the east with First Army. The objective was simple, to destroy the German Eighth Army defending that province and 'create an advantageous assembly area for further operations', which implied the capture of Berlin.

A further modification was made to the overall plan during the first week of the war. Two further armies, Ninth and Tenth, were to be created, south and east of Warsaw, which were to be used to invade Silesia with the intention of reaching Berlin even more quickly. The problem with this strategy was that it involved the Russians marching across western Poland where the infrastructure had been deliberately left underdeveloped to hinder a German/Austrian incursion from this direction. Furthermore, it was predicated on the success of SW and NW Fronts' operations not to leave its flanks exposed.

The Grand Duke Nicholas, ordered NW Front's First Army to commence operations on 15 August, to be followed three days later by Second Army.

As both forces had assembled some distance from the border several days' marches were necessary to cross the frontier. The Germans were to be outflanked; each Russian army was to move around the Masurian Lakes region, Second to the west, First to the north. The forests, swamps and lakes were superb defensive areas, particularly those to be skirted by General A.V. Samsonov's Second Army. Furthermore, the railway system favoured the Germans who would be in a position to switch troops rapidly. The danger for the Russians lay in the possibility of the two armies failing to co-ordinate the pressure they exerted and thus allowing the Germans to concentrate on one alone. In the event that is precisely what happened.

General P.K. Rennenkampf's First Army scored a victory at Gumbinnen on 20 August over three, I, XVII and I Reserve, German corps, but failed to follow up as they withdrew. Meanwhile, Second Army, led by General A.V. Samsonov, plodded forwards gradually extending its arc of advance to the west and increasing the danger of losing touch with First Army to its right. Samsonov's first contact with the Germans resulted in the capture of the town of Neidenburg on 23 August. Convinced that the Germans were retiring more rapidly than was the case, Samsonov extended his front further westwards anticipating a grand encirclement of Eighth Army. Despite Zhilinski's misgivings, this alteration to the plan was permitted. Samsonov's opposition consisted of XX Army Corps supplemented by some 15,000 Landwehr (older reserve troops) and his brief was to screen Eighth Army's right flank. The first major encounter was around the village of Orlau where, once again, the Germans advanced with bugles and banners and the result was another Russian victory. With two victories under their belts Samsonov and Rennenkampf had good reason to be pleased. However, they had not counted on German staff work and the gamble that Eighth Army's new commanders were to sanction. Fate had dealt Ludendorff and von Hindenburg, the new Chief-of-Staff and Commander of Eighth Army respectively, two good cards – the orders for Second and First armies had fallen into their hands, both from radio intercepts. The question was the validity of the latter; apparently Rennenkampf was not going to advance with any vigour if at all to link up with Samsonov's right flank. Samsonov was extending his left even further to the west and his line of advance was breaking into channels funnelled through forest, river and swamp.

The German commanders gambled and moved troops from the east to form a pocket into which it was anticipated that Second Army would march. Leaving only a cavalry screen to cover First Army, XX Army Corps' position was to be held while other formations from XVII and I corps were shuffled by foot and railway to create the flanks of the encirclement.

Samsonov, with his communications 'system' virtually non-existent, was unaware of the Germans movements until it was too late. First his left flank then his right were defeated as his centre marched forward unprotected. By the end of August Samsonov was dead and his men either POWs or routing back across the border. Rounding up the POWs and securing the area took several days, then it was to be First Army's turn to face a reinforced Eighth Army. Unaware of the scale of Second Army's collapse, Zhilinski had issued no orders to rush to its aid, while Rennenkampf digested the information that Samsonov was in retreat. The Germans attacked and by mid-September had driven First Army from German soil. East Prussia was saved for the moment.

To the south, however, the situation facing Austria was approaching catastrophic. The Austrian general staff was well aware of the fact that it would have to carry the burden of the fighting in the east until the arrival of the bulk of the German army fresh from its victory over France. However, instead of maintaining a defensive posture and letting the Russians advance, von Hotzendorf was eager to bring his opponents to battle on the plains of Galicia and gain victory in a magnificent set-piece battle (as did the majority of his contemporaries across Europe) and set off into the east screened by thousands of increasingly exhausted, saddle-sore mounts that had been forced to carry their riders on stiff parade saddles for the 'look of it'.

The first important clash took place as Krasnik in southern Poland between Russian Fourth and Austrian First armies. The Russians were defeated when attacking directly from the march, uphill. General Baron A.E. Salza withdrew to the north-east opening up a gap between his Fourth and Fifth armies. Russian concerns regarding an Austrian advance into the rear of NW Front were apparently being confirmed and troops were diverted from south of Warsaw to counter this threat. Emboldened by this victory, von Hotzendorf inclined his southern armies to encircle Pleve's Fifth Army apparently unaware of the threat posed to his rear by Third and Eighth Russian armies to the east. However, Pleve, following the defeat of part of his army at Komarov, withdrew. The resulting manoeuvres by both sides were a series of attempts to encircle one another. Attack followed by counterattack left the Austrians, by early September, increasingly vulnerable to outright defeat. Despite receiving reinforcements from the Serbian front von Hotzendorf's armies failed either to encircle or defeat the Russian advance.

Falling back behind the San River, the Austrians had themselves narrowly avoided falling into a similar trap as Samsonov. With much of Galicia occupied, the SW Front paused to refresh and reorganise before moving towards the passes through the Carpathian Mountains and into Hungary. Removing almost 100,000 Austrian POWs proved to be a considerable logistical exercise. It is no wonder that the Grand Duke Nicholas informed the Tsar, 'with extreme joy and thanking God that Lvov (Lemberg) is now ours'.

Zhilinski was replaced as commander of NW Front by General N.V. Ruzski and both he and Ivanov from SW Front appeared at a conference held at Cholm, presided over by the Grand Duke, to discuss the next step.

The results of the conference were to realign the Russian armies and to go ahead with the Silesian invasion utilising the reconstituted Second Army and elements of SW Front. Both the positions covering East Prussian and the Carpathians were to be maintained as they were. However, Germany had, ungraciously, agreed to provide support for the Austrians by advancing into Russian Poland against 'the flank and rear of the first group of armies pursuing the Austrians, towards Cracow'. Happily for Stavka a set of orders for the newly assembled German Ninth Army was discovered on a corpse on 30 September, the day after Ninth Army began its march. Three Russian armies, Fourth, Ninth and First, were ordered westwards to fall on the German's left flank while Tenth Army carried out holding attacks towards East Prussia. Unfortunately for the Russians, German intelligence received news of their movements and Ninth Army was pulled back almost 100km to its start line. However, the Austrians had managed to withdraw safely to Cracow and their lines now connected with those of their northern ally. Once again Stavka began to prepare for the Silesian invasion which was scheduled to begin on 14 November. But yet again poor radio security gifted the Germans knowledge of the Russian plan and they struck first on 11 November.

Three men of the 67th Infantry Regiment pose for the camera. The line regiments were numbered serially so this regiment was part of Second Brigade, 17th Infantry Division, XIX Army Corps. They were initially deployed as part of Fifth Army and were involved in the Battle of Komarov against the Austro-Hungarians.

An unidentified infantry regiment waits during the summer of 1914. The regimental standard, here wrapped in protective material, was carried into the field where it was closely guarded. After significant losses of regalia in 1914–15, Stavka decided to send flags and standards to the rear to replacement units, since at times two or three companies were protecting a flag or standard, and of course that decreased the firepower of Russian units. The Germans went into action at Gumbinnen with flags flying and drums beating.

Private Pavel Zherdev, dressed as millions of other Russian infantrymen in August 1914, was destined to survive the war, revolution and civil war. He rose to become a powerful local administrator in a region on the Volga River only to die during the Stalinist Purges of the 1930s.

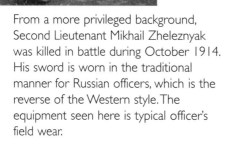

From a more privileged background, Second Lieutenant Mikhail Zheleznyak was killed in battle during October 1914. His sword is worn in the traditional manner for Russian officers, which is the reverse of the Western style. The equipment seen here is typical officer's field wear.

A Nieuport IV and pilot in flying kit. The Russian Military Air Fleet was divided into twenty-eight detachments, of six aircraft, one for each army corps. A wide variety of machines made up the 250 aircraft in use at the outbreak of the war. Of these, 145 were front-line types. Aircraft production in Russia was hampered by a lack of plants capable of manufacturing aero engines.

Russia was unique in possessing the world's only heavy bomber force – the Squadron of Flying Ships. Equipped with four-engined aircraft designed by I.I. Sikorsky and known as the *Illya Muromets*, the first group of these aircraft was based at Yablonna airfield near Warsaw in late 1914. This machine is a Type IX, at Pskov during 1916. Capable of carrying over 200kg of bombs and up to four machine guns, *Illya Muromets* carried out their first bombing mission over German lines on 15 February 1915.

In September 1914 the First Automobile Machine Gun Company was formed in Petrograd and departed for the front some months later. It was reinforced in early 1915 with this armoured Packard lorry that carries an automatic 37mm Maxim-Nordenfeldt cannon. This gun could be fired from the truck bed or from the ground on a wheeled carriage.

Across the length and breadth of the Russian empire scenes like this were enacted daily during the summer of 1914. Dignitaries, friends and family accompanied by a band see the local troops off to war. It was the first war in which Russia's new alcohol prohibition law was in place and as a consequence the traditional drunken farewells were less evident.

On 3 August the Grand Duke N.N. Romanov, second cousin of the Tsar, was appointed Supreme Commander-in-Chief. His Chief-of-Staff, General N.N. Yanushkevitch, was appointed by the Tsar not the Grand Duke: it was one of many such appointments that the Tsar would make to demonstrate his authority.

Officers of the 17th *Arkhangelogorodsky* Infantry Regiment. Part of IX Army Corps, they crossed into Austria-Hungary as part of Third Army. Their victory over the Austrians led to the fall of Lemberg, the capital of Austria's province of Galicia, on 3 September.

The route into Austria-Hungary lay across large tracts of open grassland, cut by river valleys, as this image testifies. As one Russian commentator noted, this was an area where 'large masses of troops could be manoeuvred easily but gave the Austrians no ... advantage as a defensive position'.

Marching into East Prussia during August 1914 was a gruelling business with temperatures often reaching 35 °C. Sandy soil inhibited the movement of men and wagons. Tradition dictated that Russian infantrymen in the field kept their bayonets attached. Greatcoats were carried rolled around the body, while a knapsack contained all the essentials. The central figure here carries a tent section and pole.

In the wake of the advancing armies snaked long columns of supply and casualty evacuation wagons. Many, such as this one, were pressed into service. The local *panje* wagons were versatile and when hauled by tough, small horses proved capable of traversing all terrain in all conditions.

A corps of the Silesian Landwehr, typified by the men seen here, had joined Austrian First Army on 3 September. Under the command of General Remus von Worsych, this formation of roughly 26,000 men marched virtually unopposed and undetected some 300km through Russian Poland only to suffer 30 per cent casualties covering the Austrian withdrawal from Lublin in early September.

The first recipient of the St George's Cross was Cossack Kozma Kryuchkov, an NCO in 3rd Don Cossack Cavalry Regiment, part of First Army. General Rennenkampf, First Army's commander, 'took off his St. George ribbon pinned (it) on my chest and (gave his) congratulations to the first cross of St. George'. Kryuchkov commanded a patrol that killed some twenty-four German cavalry during August 1914.

Literacy rates and newspaper circulation had increased dramatically during the decade prior to 1914 but there was heavy censorship. In a less cynical age stories of military daring-do enjoyed widespread popularity. This postcard shows Kozma Kryuchkov and describes how he won his medal. It is entitled 'First Hero'. Some of the proceeds from the sale of this item would go to soldiers' charities. His portrait also graced cigarette and sweet wrappers.

1-й Герой.

Четыре русскихъ казака,
А нѣмцевъ было тридцать два,
И вотъ одинъ казакъ Крючковъ;
Вдругъ въ кучу врѣзался враговъ,
Три остальныхъ за нимъ спѣшатъ,
И нѣмцевъ вкругъ себя крошатъ.
И вотъ чрезъ нѣсколько минутъ
Насталъ для нѣмцевъ ужъ капутъ.
Хоть и залитъ Крючковъ весь кровью,
Но не моргнетъ онъ даже бровью.
Онъ смѣло вкругъ себя рубилъ,
Одиннадцать враговъ убилъ,
И получивъ шестнадцать ранъ
Безъ помощи доѣхалъ въ станъ.
За храбрость сталъ казакъ донской

Собствен. изданіе
ФАБРИКИ
А. Ф. Постнова.
Москва. Тел. 27-75.
Перепечатка воспрещ

Unfortunately for Russia heroes were not enough. The combination of the efficiency of the German staff in East Prussia and the stolid fighting qualities of their troops were a match for the invaders.

Russian POWs in Austrian hands. At Tannenberg the Germans claimed 90,000 were captured. In 1916, through the auspices of the Red Cross, Samsonov's body was returned to his wife for burial in the family plot. The Kaiser proposed that the Russian prisoners be driven onto a barren spit of land in the Baltic and kept there till they died of thirst and hunger.

A patrol of Ulans (lancers). Austria-Hungary committed ten cavalry divisions spread across a front of 160km to find the Russians. The information gathered was of negligible value. Consequently, the men and horses were exhausted and of little use for several weeks. Austrian lancer units were such in name only being armed with carbine and sword. Uniformed in blue tunics and red trousers, they were easy targets.

At the village of Jaroslawice on 21 August Russian and Austro-Hungarian cavalry met in what proved to be a classic cavalry engagement, as depicted in this painting. Austrian 4th Cavalry Division fought Russian 10th Cavalry Division, charging and counter-charging. Finally, the Russians prevailed. Their booty included 8 guns, 4 caissons, 2 machine guns, 151 prisoners and 150 horses.

Chapter Two

Snow and Mud,
Winter 1914–Spring 1915

The pre-emptive attack launched by German Ninth Army was, at first, seen as nothing but a feint. However, when the full extent of the threat to part of the Silesian invasion force, Second and Fifth armies, became apparent Stavka reacted swiftly and in a series of running battles around Lodz the Germans were first held and then forced to withdraw but at the cost of the Silesian operation being once more put on hold.

To the south SW Front's Third and Eighth armies had been advancing steadily towards the Carpathian foothills. Furthermore, an Austrian offensive to relieve the pressure on Cracow had come to naught. Indeed, such was the Austrian perception of the threat from SW Front that plans were afoot to improve the defences around Budapest and the Danube River crossings. The threat to the Carpathian passes was posed by the advance of Third (General Radko-Dmitriev) and Eighth (General A. A. Brusilov) armies.

At a front commanders' conference on 29 November Ivanov requested more troops to clear 'the way to Berlin . . . through Austria-Hungary' and received Ninth Army. However, as these reinforcements plodded south, the Austrians struck at the point where Third and Eighth armies' link was weakest and by 10 December both had been forced to retire, the immediate threat to Hungary had been contained. Nor was the fighting in western Poland going well for the Russians as, on 19 December, Lodz fell to the Germans. Although Stavka did not admit as much, the invasion of Silesia was now off the agenda. Indeed, Ruzski reiterated his request to pull NW Front back to a line running from the Novo-Georgievsk fortress that covered Warsaw to the fortified city of Kovno to the north-east in Lithuania. This position was deep inside Russian territory and as such unacceptable to Stavka not least for the political effect such a retreat may have had on the populations of Poland and Lithuania, or Courland as it was then known.

As the snows of winter deepened and the men of all sides shivered in their ill-defined trenches it became clear that that this would not be a short, glorious war.

Some 70km behind SW Front's line lay the immense fortress complex of Przemysl in which were contained 120,000 Austrian troops. Von Hotzendorf, well aware that supplies in the fortress would run out by early March, was determined to raise the siege. However, this operation would only be possible with German support.

Falkenhayn, the new German Chief-of-Staff (effectively Commander-in-Chief) did not favour the Eastern Front but was forced into conceding that troops from the West would form part of a joint Austro-German command – Sud Armee, which was to form part of the offensive force.

Stavka also faced a dilemma – where should it launch its next operation? In the event NW Front was to create a new army, Twelfth, from reconstituted units of Samsonov's force along with corps from First and Tenth armies. Unfortunately, the demands of SW Front drew off some of the units intended for Twelfth Army with the result that neither front had sufficient forces to carry out its plans. In the case of NW Front this was to be an invasion of East Prussia from the south to begin in mid-February. SW Front's requirements were to hold off the upcoming Austrian offensive.

Von Hotzendorf's planning embraced the length of the Carpathian Mountains and began on 23 January 1915. A week's hard fighting resulted in the re-capture of a single pass and that at astronomic cost. A speedy Russian counter-offensive then promptly recaptured much of the lost ground. To the south in the more sparsely defended, relatively open Bukovina region the western bank of the Dniester River was reached. Operations then ground to a halt due to the near impossibility of doing anything but survive in the wintery landscape. Nevertheless, von Hotzendorf once again launched his men towards Przemysl. The attacks ground to a rapid halt with units sustaining up to 80 per cent casualties, mainly from frostbite and exposure, by mid-February.

It was now NW Front's turn to face an attack. Ludendorff launched Eighth and newly formed Tenth armies, on 7 February, on an ambitious pincer movement designed to encircle Russian Tenth Army before it could co-operate with the still-assembling Twelfth Army. Tragically for Russian Tenth army its warnings of German activity were ignored by Ruzski at Front HQ. Within four days Tenth Army's right flank had all but disintegrated in the face of German attacks. However, much of Eighth Army's strength was drawn into a series of futile attacks on the strongly entrenched little Russian fortress of Osowiec which held out. As the German advance dragged itself through waist-deep snow, Russian Twelfth Army came into play. Alongside Tenth Army, it pushed the Germans back into East Prussia but it was too late for Ruzski and in early March he was replaced by General M.V. Alexeyev, formerly Chief-of-Staff at SW Front.

If Stavka believed that Alexeyev would be more sympathetic to the needs of SW

Front and to the Grand Duke Nicholas' aspirations for a renewed offensive against the Austrians, they were to be proved wrong. Alexeyev was as begrudging of troops as his predecessor and dispatched only one first-line corps along with several second-line divisions towards the creation of the new Ninth Army along the Dniester River near the Romanian border. Happily for Ivanov, the fall of Przemysl released more troops. It was with these newly acquired reinforcements that SW Front was to 'Complete the ruin of Austria-Hungary'. What Ivanov had been wary of, as both the Austrians and Germans had learnt to their cost during their recent operations, was the danger of outrunning supply lines. Ground could be taken but it could not be held if the wherewithal to do so was lacking.

Before Christmas the Russian gunners had been firing off more shells than had been imagined possible six months earlier. The introduction of the Great Programme of 1913 had dismissed the possibility of a long war and had presumed that the stocks of ammunition, 1,000 rounds per gun, would be sufficient for all eventualities. This did not prove to be the case for Russia or any of the other nations involved, which held similar stockpiles based on a similar philosophy. Russia's initial response when reality dawned was to order from overseas suppliers to make good the shortfall in domestic production. Unfortunately, other nations were doing precisely the same but the lack of suppliers was not Russia's only problem. With the Black and Baltic seas closed to Russian ships, the empire had been reduced to three accessible ports, Archangel, Vladivostok and Murmansk. Of these, Archangel was iced up from October to May: only Murmansk, which lacked a railhead, and Vladivostok, at the end of the 9,300km, mainly single track, Trans-Siberian Railway that ran to Moscow, were ice free. In late 1914 work began on a line to connect Murmansk to its nearest railhead 1,100km to the south from where it would link to Petrograd. Archangel was the terminus for 560km of narrow-gauge track which then connected to the main gauge. However, neither of these projects would be completed until 1916 because of the horrendous terrain through which they would run. Consequently, it fell to the Russian government to step up production at the State arsenals and encourage private industry to enter the munitions sector. During the course of 1915 both these aspirations were achieved.

Unfortunately, during the months of shortage problems arose, although not on the scale claimed by some contemporary writers. Overall the Germans generally and the Austrians consistently were outnumbered by the Russians in terms of artillery. It was not until 1916 that the Russian artillery came into its own by which time the domestic industrial base was providing more than enough shell for even the most profligate bombardment.

The failure of the Austrians to relieve Przemysl had convinced von Hotzendorf that the grandiose scheme of linking up with the Germans east of Warsaw was now a fantasy beyond his armies' powers. Indeed, it was about just within their capacity to hold the slowly building offensive by SW Front. On paper Ivanov's command numbered forty-one divisions, but many were under strength. Brusilov's Eighth Army was so worn out that he simply wanted to hold, 'with as few losses as possible'. These factors aside the Russian offensive, slow though it was, triggered a response from the Germans who set about providing not only sufficient troops to reinforce the Carpathian Front but for an offensive in great force.

As the Germans moved men eastwards, Ivanov mounted a series of short, stabbing attacks through the valleys isolating mountain and hill-top garrisons and forcing them to surrender. The Austrians held on convinced that retreat would open up the way to Hungary and the disaster that would ensue when recruiting grounds and the imperial breadbasket fell into Russian hands. On 6 April Ludendorff sent the newly formed *Beskid Korps*, named after the area in which they would fight, to the aid of the Austrians. Its arrival coincided with SW Front reaching the end of its supply capabilities and the Russian offensive was halted on 10 April. During the days that followed more and more German reinforcements poured into the 90km-front facing Third Army. General Radko-Dmitriev's command, which linked Fourth and Eighth armies, had hardly moved for several months. The left flank of Third Army ran into the foothills of the Carpathians where it connected with Eighth Army, while its right went into Poland where it connected with Fourth Army. Its centre was the 35km-stretch between the towns of Tarnow to the north and Gorlice to the south. However, intelligence gathered from various sources, including Russian fliers, regarding the enemy build-up was dismissed. In some respects Radko-Dmitriev had grounds for optimism: the Easter truce had just passed off without incident and his 650 guns reported adequate supplies of shell. Urged into doing so, he ordered his men to begin digging support and communications trenches immediately before leaving his HQ for a celebration for the St George's Order.

The order was carried out with little enthusiasm as the officers and men of Third Army assumed they would be going over to the offensive in a short time. Entrenching tools were in short supply and the assignment of men to working parties was viewed as endangering the security of the front line. Two corps, IX and X, held the positions at the junction with Fourth Army and they were to be the first target. Both these corps were made up of first-line troops and their ranks were certainly not packed with poor quality conscripts.

On the left, dressed in Circassian uniform, General A.A. Brusilov, commander of SW Front's Eighth Army, and to the right, General N.V. Ruzski, formerly commander of Third Army.

Russian cavalry riding through the snow and mud of Poland. At this stage of the war large areas of the front were merely covered by cavalry patrols or companies of local territorials. As the front in France and Belgium degenerated into trench warfare, in the east manoeuvre was still an option, although the distances involved almost precluded any far-flung flanking moves.

An Austrian supply column wends its way into one of the Carpathian passes during the winter of 1914–15. Infantry attacks in this region were ghastly affairs. Contemporary accounts note men wading waist high through as the blood from wounds coloured the snow pink. Morale in the Hapsburg armies plummeted as the casualty list rocketed.

The fortress of Przemysl had been cut off from the main Austrian line twice before it was formally besieged in autumn 1914. However, initially the Russians lacked a train of siege guns with which to bombard the concrete and earth fortifications. When such were allocated from naval guns stored with the Baltic Fleet and the fortress of Brest Litovsk it took weeks to move them into place as they lacked field carriages.

German *uhlans* (lancers) ride through the snow, February 1915. On the Eastern Front cavalry played a more significant role than in the West because of the greater length of front to be covered. The ability of such formations to ride around exposed flanks and penetrate the rear echelons of the enemy often gave rise to panic and rumour of greater danger than actually existed.

On the left a man of a reserve division and on the right a member of the *opolchenie* (local, home-guard units), who were distinguished by the cross on their forage caps above the imperial cockade. Neither troop types were highly regarded by the senior staff as they were believed to be poorly trained, lacking in motivation and unreliable. Increasingly pressed into front-line duty, particularly on SW Front, such formations were called upon to perform tasks for which they were unsuited. They often lacked artillery, modern rifles and machine guns let alone modern field kit and clothing, as the *opolchenie* man seen here clearly demonstrates.

The German units transferred to the East during the winter of 1914–15 were combat veterans who were to prove themselves time and again in this theatre during the course of the spring and summer. Many of the Russian recruits assigned to SW Front's reserve and *opolchenie* formations were newly conscripted men from the recently conquered Austro-Hungarian territory of Galicia whose military experience, if any, was in the Hapsburg armies of a decade before the war.

The large numbers of men called to the colours caused shortages of weapons both at the front and in the training depots. Consequently, regiments were ordered to establish repair facilities close to the line to maintain rifles and other weapons. The workshop of the 99th *Ivangorodsky* Infantry Regiment is seen here. A further incentive was the payment of a bounty to men who recovered weapons from the battlefield.

Russian troops demonstrate a variety of gas masks available in 1917. The first use of gas on the Eastern Front took place near the Polish village of Bolimov, some 60km west of Warsaw, on 31 January 1915. The gas used was xylyl bromide, a tear gas, which failed because of the sub-zero temperature into which it was released by the use of gas-filled shells.

A fire-swept height in the Carpathian Mountains with shattered trees providing scant protection to the barely visible defensive positions. In was in such areas that much of the fighting between Austrian and Russian forces took place. It is easy to imagine the problems presented to the men told off for ammunition carrying.

The bleak, yet relatively open terrain of the Bukovina dwarfs the Russian supply convoy just visible on the road in the centre of the image. Russian horses were far more capable of surviving in such harsh conditions than their counterparts serving the Austro-German armies.

Casualty evacuation from the Carpathians and elsewhere on the Eastern Front was often carried out by a local farmer's vehicle, in this case a *panje* wagon fitted with runners to cross snow. Unfortunately for this Austrian, casualty movement is impeded by the slush in the town.

Conditions were no better for the Russians. During the early part of 1915 many voluntary organisations and wealthy individuals began to provide practical help, such as hospital trains, and financial support to the overstretched medical facilities of the army. Local and regional governments across Russia commandeered buildings for use as hospitals that were then staffed by volunteers.

Realising that relief was not coming, the garrison of Przemysl attempted to break out on 20 March but failed due to stiff Russian opposition. Demolition of the major fortifications began the following day. The surrender of Przemysl on 22 March 1915 released the resources of Eleventh Army (General A.N. Selivanov). However, the majority of these troops were reserves or, as seen here, *opolchenie*. The Austrians lost 100,000 POWs and vast stocks of munitions.

To those accustomed to the close proximity of the opposing trench systems in the West the situation in the East came as a great surprise. In several sectors of Third Army's front the lines were up to 3km apart. Life for the locals continued almost as normal. Indeed, many made money from both sides by providing information on the other's activities.

Barbed wire was at a premium in 1915 and other methods of defence were widespread, as seen here. Along Third Army's front the defences were thin to say to the least.

Here a group of officers amuse themselves with the mock execution of a spy. The Russians were particularly suspicious of the Jews who they believed to be acting as agents for the Central Powers who allowed them more rights than the Tsar's regime. That Third Army ignored such information as it received would result in dire consequences in the early days of May 1915.

Chapter Three

Heavy Metal Thunder

In a report that should have generated more of a response than it did Third Army's Chief-of-Staff noted precisely that the Germans meant to 'break through at Novysacz . . .'. At 0600hr on 2 May the German and Austrian artillery began to hammer at the Russian line between Gorlice and Tarnow. Third Army's guns were still in the positions they had occupied during weeks of desultory Austrian shelling. Although the Russians may have been contemptuous of their Austrian counterparts' efforts now, the enemy proved their point as the Russian batteries were blown to pieces with little or no work required to find the range for this had already been done. The infantry in their sketchy trenches fared even worse. With their amateurish defences in ruins, their comrades reduced to tattered bundles of rags or screaming in agony, the shell-shocked, deafened survivors were in no condition to fight and simply raised their arms and capitulated.

For two days the Germans advanced, brushing aside poorly organised counterattacks until they were brought up short by the lack of supplies and the tough resistance of III Caucasian Corps. To the south and left of Third Army Russia's Eighth Army began to retire, sacrificing much of its XXIV Corps in a futile counterattack on the German right flank. Ivanov, SW Front's commander, now requested that he be allowed to withdraw to the San River which he believed to be the best defensible line. Six days later permission was granted for Third Army to retire to the river but by this time it was so weak that it was doubtful if it could even hold the San line. To its right Brusilov's Eighth Army had withdrawn its right to include the echoing ruins of Przemysl fortress. Simultaneously, Eleventh Army pulled back.

Paradoxically, while the other armies of SW Front fell back, Ninth Army was advancing against the Austrians in the Bukovina province down by the Romanian frontier. Nor was the Central Powers' Sud-Armee having much success against Eleventh Army. However, all Falkenhayn's efforts were concentrated on breaking the Russians along the San River. Reinforcements, including the Prussian Guard Corps, fresh stocks of ammunition and other supplies were pushed forward. Indeed, the German Supreme HQ was transferred to Pless in Silesia and the Kaiser himself arrived, anxious to witness what was hoped would be the attack that would 'cripple permanently the Russian offensive strength'.

In mid-May, following another mighty barrage, one German and one Austrian corps overran a Russian bridgehead on the San River at Radymno and, crossing on the heels of the fleeing Russians, established their own footing on the right bank.

A second crossing followed to the north on 19 May. However, further south both Austrian Third Army and the Sud-Armee's efforts were held by counterattacks and ferocious defensive fighting. German forces were diverted to this region and this slowed down operations in the Przemysl region. Despite this, it was decided to abandon the ruins of this once-mighty fortress which was reoccupied by the Austrians on 4 June when Brusilov pulled out the skeleton garrison.

On 25 May 1915 Italy declared war on Austria-Hungary. Nevertheless, von Hotzendorf and Falkenhayn agreed to continue the aggressive policy in the East against SW Front. Despite part of Austrian Third Army being sent to Italy, the San River remained the theatre of choice. Army Group Mackensen, German Eleventh Army, flanked left and right by Austrian Fourth and Second armies respectively, was now ordered to drive eastwards towards Rawa-Ruska and Lvov.

Once again the sledgehammer blows of the Austro-German gunners pounded the lines of Third Army. On 15 June after three days of hard fighting a wedge was driven between Third and Eighth armies. Now the Russians began a full-scale retreat, Third Army to the north-east, Eighth, Ninth and Eleventh armies to the east. Luckily for the Russians, the Austro-German forces advanced steadily and were unable to exploit the potentially deadly gap between the armies.

As the problems of SW Front grew in seriousness, Grand Duke Nicholas chaired a conference, on 17 June, at which both front commanders counselled a withdrawal to shorten the 1,700km-line and using the divisions thus released to form a significant reserve. Galicia was to be abandoned but Poland defended by means of the fortress system established for just that purpose, after all, they reasoned, had not Ossoviets and Ivangorod held firm against previous attacks? Novo-Georgievsk, the greatest of the Polish bastions, was anticipated to prove equal to Przemysl. But matters moved forward before a binding decision was reached. The prestigious trophy city Lemberg fell to the Austrians on 22 June. As a result of the fall of Lemberg and in light of the worsening situation an Extraordinary Council of Ministers meeting, chaired by the Tsar, was held at Stavka at Baranovitchi. Here retirement to a line running from the Gulf of Riga through Kovno and Brest Litovsk (another great fortress) to the Dniester River on the Romanian border was tabled. The Grand Duke Nicholas was vehemently opposed to the idea of abandoning so much territory but sadly for him the initiative still lay with the Central Powers who were already redeploying their forces for a series of offensives on an altogether more ambitious scale.

There were to be three attacks, one each in Lithuania, Galicia and Poland. These were to be aimed at Riga, Brest Litovsk and Warsaw in turn with mid-July scheduled as the jumping off date for all three.

Earlier in the spring a strong force of German cavalry had been launched into Courland (Lithuania). Stavka, keen to preserve the naval base at Libau against the advice of Alexeyev, then NW Front commander, ordered him to support the frontier guards and *opolchenie* battalions that held the Niemen River line from Kovno fortress to the Baltic coast. This force, noted on HQ maps as Sixth Army, was a notional army but tasked with the defence of not only Libau but also Riga, a large naval base and important industrial centre as well as a key point on the road to Petrograd. It was these factors that drove Stavka to insist on Alexeyev increasing the forces there. Despite this, Libau fell and NW Front suffered a defeat on 23 July at Shavle, roughly halfway between Riga and Kovno. Around Shavle Russian Fifth Army (General A.E. Phleve) had abandoned the city and fallen back to more defensible positions, and while it was doing so the siege of Kovno had begun. As more Russian troops were moved into the area, they gradually built up a numerical superiority. However, NW Front now had more pressing concerns than the province of Courland as Warsaw itself was under threat, as was the whole of Russian Poland.

On 18 July German Twelfth Army (General von Gallwitz) attacked the northern flank of the Polish salient near Warsaw. When the Germans broke through Alexeyev was granted permission to retreat behind the Vistula River and, if necessary, evacuate Warsaw. For the next two weeks the Russians withdrew in good order. Warsaw and the fortress of Ivangorod both fell, and the latter was comprehensively destroyed by its defenders. Ossoviets fortress stubbornly held out, acting as the hinge on which the Russian retirement in northern Poland depended. To the south in Galicia Ivanov's SW Front embarked on a similarly slow-moving retreat until they waited on good ground and gave battle up to the point that retirement was again necessary. Both Lublin and Cholm had been lost to them by the end of the month.

Amidst this generally orderly sea of retreat the fortress of Novo-Georgievsk was expected to prove a rock of defiance behind German lines to the north of Warsaw. Novo-Georgievsk was to be formally invested by a force under General von Beseler, who had destroyed the defences of Antwerp in 1914 and now, accompanied by a formidable siege train, most of which outranged the fortress guns, he was prepared to repeat his Belgian performance. The capture of the fort's senior engineer with a complete set of plans gave von Beseler the upper hand from the first day. The garrison surrendered after three days of mind-boggling bombardment on 20 August. The Germans claimed 90,000 officers and men as POWs, including 30 generals and 1,600 guns taken.

The Central Powers' advance into Poland, Galicia and the Baltic provinces was not a cheaply bought success. By late August von Gallwitz was providing casualty returns of 30 per cent. Clean, drinkable water was difficult to come by and other necessaries were also in short supply. By this time Ludendorff concluded, '[We] can probably force the Russians to retreat but not to a decisive end.' With the abandonment of the fortress complex of Brest Litovsk on 26 August and the advance against SW Front reaching the vast wetlands of the Pripet Marshes, the Polish salient was now flattened out. Falkenhayn turned his attention to the destruction of Serbia but Ludendorff wished to maintain pressure on Russia's Baltic provinces. To this end, he launched an operation aimed at capturing Vilna. Frontal attacks on the city failed badly, incurring heavy losses, but an attack to the north found a gap and on 18 September the city was taken at the cost of 45,000 casualties.

There was no possibility of a great encirclement as von Hotzendorf and the Austrians had hoped for and nor did the Russians sue for peace as Falkenhayn had dreamt. However, it was the collapse of the fortress system and particularly the loss of Kovno on 18 August that galvanised the Russian government, personified by the Tsar, into what was tantamount to a flurry of activity. On 26 June General A.A. Polivanov had been appointed War Minister, replacing the disgraced Sukhomlinov, and other changes were to follow. At roughly the same time the Special Council was formed which took over all aspects of military supply from the hands of the War Minister. Consisting of Duma members and leading industrialists, it was to have a profoundly positive effect on the already rapidly modernising Russian domestic armaments industry. Although the front had contracted from 1,700km to just over 1,000km, it was decided to divide it into three fronts, the Northern, the Western and the South-Western presided over by generals Ruzski, Evert and Ivanov respectively. Alexeyev had been promoted to Chief-of-Staff to the Supreme Commander-in-Chief but it was no longer the Grand Duke Nicholas who held that post. Factions in the military, the government, the bureaucracy and the court led by the Tsaritsa herself had been working towards his fall. His replacement was none other than the Tsar himself. Having no military experience, Nicholas II viewed himself as a figurehead, a symbol that would bind the Russian people in some mystical fashion to the prosecution of the war. Taking up his 'burden' on 1 September, Nicholas' self-appointment coincided neatly with the running down of the Central Powers' offensive. It only remained for the Austrians to mount a final, independent push in the south. However, it failed and required support to prevent Brusilov's Eighth Army from holding onto the important railway junction of Lutsk. On 26 September Ludendorff called a halt to operations and ordered his men to dig in and consolidate, while the Tsar and Alexeyev established their new HQ at the town of Mogilev. The so-called Great

Retreat was over. Falkenhayn, with no desire to repeat Napoleon's experience of 1812–13, had contained the ambitions of Hindenburg, Ludendorff and von Hotzendorf. However, the European theatre was not the only one that Russia had to consider.

The Gorlice–Tarnow Operation was under the leadership of General August von Mackensen. His command included German Eleventh Army and Austrian Fourth and Third armies. The assembly of heavy artillery included several batteries of 305mm Skoda mortars, as seen here. Eleventh Army led the offensive with the Austrians on its flanks.

Third Army POWs under German guard. During May 1915 Rako-Dmitriev's command lost over 140,000 POWs and 200 guns. IX Corps commander stated, 'territorial troops have been utterly feeble, surrendering in droves'.

The poor quality of the Russian defences is clearly seen here. The sandy nature of the soil was also a hindrance. Materiel, such as barbed wire, tools and pit props, captured from the Austrians at Przemysl, had been sold off to local farmers earlier in the year.

Not all went well for the Central Powers. The Austrians in the centre suffered a significant reverse in late May and many thousands were captured while retreating until supported by German troops and artillery. However, later tales of mass surrenders by disaffected Hapsburg subjects were grossly distorted as such events were rare.

With the largest air force in the East the Russians were well aware of the dangers posed by aircraft, certainly in terms of bombing and reconnaissance. This anti-aircraft position allows for 360 degrees of traverse and is one of several that would have provided a heavy rate of fire.

August von Mackensen was promoted to Field Marshal on 22 June 1915 for his successes against SW Front, particularly the recapture of Lemberg. He commanded various forces on the Eastern Front throughout the war and was finally captured by the Serbs in 1918.

As the gap between Eighth and Third Russian armies grew it was patrolled by elements of three cavalry divisions. However, as Brusilov noted, 'It is obvious to anyone that three cavalry divisions, though they may be heroically disposed cannot take the place of four Army Corps.' Here an officer of a Caucasian Cossack unit is buried with full ceremony.

Austrian cavalry question locals as to the whereabouts of the Russians. The complete lack of metalled roads inevitably turned the tracks into bottomless mud and held up the advance of the Central Powers' supply lines.

During the Russian retreat prepared positions were few and far between. Here a battery of howitzers, Schneider M1910 122mm pieces, poses for the camera in drill positions in the open.

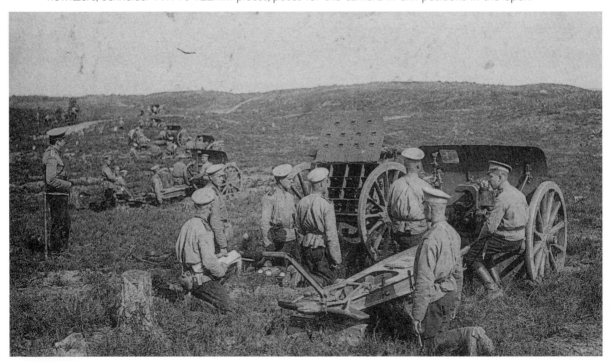

German artillerymen sit astride one of the immense, immobile guns captured at Novo-Georgievsk during the summer of 1915. However, the majority of the regimental flags were flown out by the pilots of the garrison to avoid further humiliation.

German soldiers hunt for souvenirs in the ruins of the fortress at Przemysl. Such was the destruction wrought before the Austrian surrender in March 1915 the Russians found themselves in possession of little but ruins to defend.

German dragoons wait to cross the Niemen River into Courland. This area was weakly defended by local units, which were poorly armed and inadequately led. A large German cavalry force led the advance towards the vital railway junction of Molodetchno in September 1915 failed badly as units were unable to support one another and suffered heavy casualties while withdrawing.

A member of the *opolchenie* poses with his wife. When he was called to fight it was likely that she would join the 2,000,000 refugees that streamed eastwards during the summer of 1915. Many of the refugees were Jewish as vast swathes of the Pale of Settlement (an area of Russian Poland set aside especially for the Jewish population) were lost to the Tsar. The forcible evacuation of Jews, regarded as untrustworthy by the imperial authorities, led to many atrocities as the Russian troops were not prevented from venting their spleen on an ethnic group perceived as deserving of such treatment.

From 20 May 1915 various categories of *opolchenie* began to be called to the colours. These locally raised units were dressed in what the territorial government had available, such as the old pattern tunics seen here. The bronze cross on their caps shows they are militia.

The gates of the State-owned Tula arsenal in pre-war days. During 1915 the manufacture of all kinds of munitions had risen dramatically. Overcoming bureaucratic suspicions of private enterprise was a slow process but bore fruit that year. Field-gun shell production rose from 350,000 to over 1,500,000 per month between January and November 1915. State funding of industry was gradually increased over the next twelve months and munitions began to flow in vast quantities.

That there were not widespread epidemics in the Russian hinterland in the wake of the refugees' arrival was due in great part to the work of charities, urban and provincial authorities. These bodies organised food and medical supplies on a huge scale and alleviated much suffering. The women seen here are selling favours such as flags of the allies to raise funds for the Red Cross.

To replace the losses among experienced NCOs special schools had been established during 1915. A group from one such school is seen here. It was also decided that enlisted men would spend less time in the rear areas and move to their units at the front to learn more about modern warfare. It was equally important to remove recruits from the malign influence of political agitators. Fast-track courses for junior officers had been initiated earlier due to the horrific casualties experienced in 1914.

As the front settled down lines of communications were established. The soldier here is wearing puttees and ankle boots as huge stocks of leather had been lost when the tanning industry in the Baltic provinces had been overrun.

The Tsar taking control of the armed forces was greeted with mirth in Germany. Here Nicholas II seeks solace in drink as German cavalry menace the Kremlin. The verse reads, 'Nikolaus, Nikolaus, dare to leave Moscow, with our sabres, we make Russian salad, out of you.'

Nikolaus! Nikolaus!
Wag Dir blos aus
          Moskau raus!
Mit den Säbeln machen wir
Russischen Salat aus Dir.

In Petrograd the Tsaritsa, pictured here with her son on the rear steps of the Winter Palace, took on an increasingly powerful position with regards to domestic policy. As a German she was viewed with growing suspicion by many of her subjects.

Chapter Four

Snow, Stone and Sand – the Caucasian Front, 1914-17

The transfer of the Grand Duke Nicholas to the Caucasian Front provided him with face-saving prestige and the Tsar with distance from a perceived rival for power. The Grand Duke arrived at his HQ in Tiflis, capital of the Russian province of Georgia, on 24 September 1915 and his presence there immediately raised the profile of this hitherto almost forgotten front.

From the late eighteenth century the Russians had steadily driven the Turks and Persians from their Caucasian territories and the borders of 1914 were finally established in 1878. The long-term goal of successive Russian governments was the occupation of Constantinople and control of the Straits to give them access and ingress from their warm-water ports on the Black Sea. Planning for an amphibious assault on Constantinople had featured in many Russian staff discussions for over a decade before the outbreak of war and the expansion of the Black Sea Fleet was a clear indicator or Petrograd's ambitions.

Russia was in no doubt that the Ottoman Empire would join in a general European war and indeed seems to have relished the prospect of an opportunity to crush the Turks and expand their empire and sphere of influence in Asia Minor, the Middle East and Persia. Consequently, in late July 1914 General N.N. Yanushkevitch, Chief-of-Staff of the Army of the Caucasus, secretly mobilised his forces. Turkish mobilisation and the closure and mining of the Straits followed on 2 August, the day on which the Turks signed a secret alliance with Germany. The acquisition of two powerful German warships gave the Ottoman navy a distinct edge over the Russian Black Sea Fleet, which was still in the process of building capital ships. As predicted by Russia's ambassador to Constantinople, in the early hours of 29 October the Turco-German fleet bombarded Odessa and other Russian ports. On 2 November the Tsar declared war on the Sultan.

The Army of the Caucasus consisted of I–III Caucasian army corps, although only I Army Corps remained in theatre by November 1914, the others having been sent to the European front. Reinforcements began to arrive in the shape of II Turkestan

Army Corps and several Cossack infantry units. Volunteers from the local Georgian and Armenian populations were also accepted into battalion-sized formations. In total, Russian forces numbered 100,000 infantry and 15,000 cavalry (mainly Cossacks) with 256 guns.

The terrain was some of the most inhospitable in the Middle East. From the mountains of the Caucasus the ground sloped downwards into Turkish Armenia in a series of wave-like ridges between 1,500m and 3000m high.

Interspersed with fertile river valleys inhabited by peasant farmers were barren, treeless ranges of hills and large areas of semi-desert wilderness. Towns were few and far between, as were metalled roads, and rail links were non-existent. This was ground where the possibilities for outflanking moves were certainly possible if the logistical support was there. Furthermore, it was ideal for cavalry raiding.

The opening move was made by the Russians who, on 2 November, crossed the border to occupy strategic points. Outnumbered, the Turks retired but their pursuers fell into an ambush losing 7,000 men over a period of two weeks as they withdrew. All the while the Turks were assembling their forces under the control of Third Army at the fortress city of Erzurum, some 80km from the border. It was from this base that the Ottomans would conduct their Caucasian campaign, the aim of which was to restore their power in the Caucasus and their influence in Persia. Flushed with their first victory, Turkey's Commander-in-Chief, Enver Pasha, travelled to Erzurum to take personal control of operations. Enver's plan was simple, to capture Oltu and Ardahan, invade Georgia and take Kars, control of which would cut half of the Russian forces off from their base. Simultaneously, efforts would be made to raise rebellion among the Tsar's Moslem subjects in the Caucasus who had never been completely subjugated. To secure the road to Kars it was essential to take the town of Sarikamish. When the commander of Third Army was informed of Enver's plan to invade Russia in winter he promptly resigned in disgust. Despite this the Turks began their campaign on 22 December, by which time it had been snowing for two days. Nevertheless, Oltu fell on 23 December.

Within 48 hours of taking its first steps the Turkish force began to disintegrate, and marching into the teeth of blizzards the men began to drop from exposure. Meanwhile, confused intelligence had caused massive problems for the Russians at Tiflis as news of the loss of Oltu and other Turkish advances reached HQ. However, in Sarikamish 2,000 *opolchenie*, supported by 1,000 railway workers and 500 frontier guards with 2 field guns, took up defensive positions as the Turks prepared to attack. Anticipating reinforcements, the defenders of Sarikamish held on bravely, fighting off wave after wave of Turkish attackers from 26 December. Within four days the Turks had suffered 50 per cent casualties, thousands dying from exposure, and on 30

December Enver called off the attack. However, Russian HQ had different information, and according to their sources Sarikamish and Ardahan had been captured and consequently orders were issued to evacuate Tiflis. Chaos ensued as Christians, fearful of Moslem behaviour, mobbed the trains until the order was rescinded when news of the Turkish disaster at Sarikamish filtered through. Of the 120,000 men who had crossed into Russia less than 10 days before 75,000 were *hors de combat* and over 250 guns had been lost. The savage wintry conditions prevented a thorough-going pursuit, as did 28,000 Russian casualties, of which almost half were suffering from frostbite. With Oltu back in Russian hands, Yudenitch, now effectively commander of all Russian forces in the region, set about rebuilding his units and establishing the logistical network that was essential if offensive operations were to be undertaken. Road building began, mules and camels were bought by the thousand and the cavalry increased to 35,000 men. Back at Erzurum, Enver watched the shattered remnants of the army straggle in and awaited reinforcements from the west to start operations again. Given the season, little was to happen for some time.

A Turkish incursion into Persian Azerbaijan provoked a Russian response. However, it was the uprising of the Christian Armenians near Lake Van that drew Russian forces in that direction. On 14 April 1915 Armenians and other Christian groups took possession of the city of Van, which was then besieged by Turkish gendarmes. A Russian relief force entered the city on 31 May much to the joy of its defenders. With the Army of the Caucasus now increased in numbers to 150,000 infantry, mainly locally recruited volunteers, with 340 guns it was time to go over to the offensive. But the Turks had also built up their forces despite the Allied landings at Gallipoli. Some 7 infantry and 1 cavalry divisions, numbering 70,000 men, were gathering west of Lake Van as the Special Group of the Third Army. The regulars were supported by thousands of irregular Kurdish horsemen. Unfortunately for Yudenitch, his intelligence had dramatically underestimated this force. Although Russian troops occupied several towns west of Lake Van, they were unable to storm the Turks' main defences along the Belican Hills west of the town of Malazgirt. The newly formed IV Caucasian Army Corps undertaking this operation was attacked on both flanks and on 23 July forced to retreat. Other Russo-Armenian forces were now in danger of encirclement and also pulled back first towards Van and then to the Persian border. Van and Malazgirt were both reoccupied by the Turks who now advanced on a broad front. Accompanied by thousands of Christian refugees, the Russian force was only saved from disaster by the timely attack of General N.N. Baratov on the Turkish left. The reformed IV Caucasian Army Corps now threatened the Turkish right, forcing their entire front to withdraw once again and cede Van.

The difficulties of campaigning in south-western Asia Minor were clear to both sides and Yudenitch determined to focus his efforts in a more supportable area – the road to Erzurum.

To draw Turkish eyes from his preparations for the Erzurum offensive, Yudenitch, with the Grand Duke's approval, despatched Baratov with 8,000 cavalry, 6,000 infantry and 30 guns into northern Persia as an illustration of Russian power and to quell any Turco-German efforts to draw the Persians into the war on their side. This grand demonstration was carried out with great aplomb, overawing Kurds and Persians alike.

Serious preparations for the attack on Erzurum began in November 1915. As Serbia had been overrun and the Allies' Gallipoli Front was running down, speed was of the essence as the former would allow the easy flow of munitions to Turkey from the Central Powers and the latter would release men and guns for use against the Russians. Consequently, Yudenitch planned his advance to begin during the Orthodox Christmas period of 7–14 January 1916.

The Turkish Third Army held a strong position, the Koprukoy Line, that ran roughly 120km between the Pontic Alps on the left near the Black Sea coast and the Bingol Dag Mountains (some of which rose to 3,000m) on the right – it was brutal terrain. The initial Russian attack was to be against the Turkish left at the junction of XI and X army corps. To cover their preparations the Russians cloaked themselves in subterfuge. Christmas leave for all ranks was granted, reinforcements came in only at night, winter shelters were extensively and obviously constructed and rumours spread about an offensive to the east into Persia. No Russian officer below the rank of divisional commander was party to any of the planning.

The Koprukoy Line was garrisoned from left to right by X, XI and IX army corps, numbering approximately 65,000 men supported by 120 guns. To the south, to cover against a possible Russian outflanking movement, one infantry, one cavalry division and twenty battalions of gendarmes and frontier guards with a host of Kurdish irregular cavalry waited. On a map the Turkish position looked strong but it was brittle. Machine-gun nests had been dynamited out of rock, as had miles of trenches but communications were poor and the rapid movement of reserves was well-nigh impossible due to the lack of good roads. Although it would be a difficult position to break once a breach was made, it would be almost impossible to save.

With the Grand Duke's grudging permission, the attack on the Turkish left began on 10 January 1916. It achieved little, and a second only generated heavy casualties, but finally, on 13 January, the Turks committed their reserves for a counterattack and then Yudenitch unleashed his main attack.

The following day the Turkish line was breached and began to crack along its entire length and the troops fell back in good order. Yudenitch replaced his 11,000 casualties from local resources and ordered an attack in the south towards

Malazgirt, along with a push along the coast towards Trebizond. Now both the Turk's extreme flanks were under pressure. Strong reinforcements were on their way from Constantinople but would have to march some 500km from the most easterly railhead at Ankara and were not expected to arrive until April. Yudenitch was not prepared to wait as Erzurum's 15 front-line forts, supported by a second ring of 4 and a final group of 6 supported by trenches and wire entanglements, required a garrison of 75,000 and was currently held by less than two-thirds of that number. Erzurum's defences boasted 1,000 guns but less than 1 in 5 could be classified as modern. Nevertheless, it would be no easy prize as the Russians lacked heavy guns and the Turks enjoyed an exceptional reputation as defensive fighters.

From 1400hr on 11 February the Russians mounted a series of diversionary attacks which led the garrison to misplace their reserves. Within four days aerial reconnaissance indicated that the Turks were evacuating the city, which was occupied by 16 February. Cossack cavalry pursued the retreating columns for over 80km. To the south the Belican Line broke and the city of Mus was taken.

Equally successful were the combined operations along the Black Sea coastline where ships of the Russian navy helped Cossack infantry advance up to 80km to take the port of Rise, less than 50km east of Trebizond. On 19 April Trebizond was captured, signalling the end of the Russian offensive. Once again Yudenitch began the painstaking reorganisation of his forces, the securing of his rear areas and the building of a series of railway supported supply dumps, all massively time-consuming tasks.

However, by this time the Third Army had received its reinforcements and gathered up stragglers and deserters to the point where it was possible to consider a counterattack to recapture Erzurum. As they advanced, the Turks assigned some 60,000 men to recapture Trebizond. However, by late June they had made little progress as food was virtually unobtainable and munitions were in short supply. On 2 July Yudenitch counterattacked. Threatened with encirclement, Third Army began to pull back having lost 25,000 men over the course of 6 weeks. However, to the south Turkish Second Army had, on 6 August, re-taken Mus but was unable to advance any further. The area in which they were engaged had been scoured the previous year and depopulated by the ethnic cleansing the Christians had undergone and consequently no food was available. Unable to even feed their men, the Turks abandoned Mus.

The first snows of the Anatolian winter fell on 25 September and that, combined with both sides' need to reorganise, led to a suspension of hostilities. As an Austrian observer stated, 'It may be considered that both Turkish armies were, by the end of the winter, in such a state that they would not have been able to resist any serious Russian attack.' However, it was not to be.

The revolution of March 1917 ended the Caucasian campaign almost immediately. The Turks then sat and awaited events while the Russians did much the same. Georgia and the Russian territories of Azerbaijan and Armenia began to petition for independence and form their own armed forces based on units in the Army of the Caucasus. With the coming of the armistice on 15 December 1917 the Russian troops simply packed up and left for home and the civil war. Now facing only a variety of well-armed but disparate local formations, the Turks' patience was rewarded as they reoccupied Erzurum and prepared to invade the Caucasus. For Baratov's near-forgotten force in Persia the revolutions of 1917 opened the doors on a series of adventures that require a book of their own.

The Tsar reviews units of the Caucasian Army, late 1914. To replace troops sent to fight Austria and Germany Nicholas found it necessary to sanction the recruitment of large numbers of Georgians and Armenians into his army, although Russian policy was set against such nationalist formations. In the event they proved loyal, hardy fighters.

General Yudenitch, third from right, proved to be one of Russia's most effective leaders. Far from industrial resources, he made the most of his assets and fought a careful, well-thought-out campaign.

One of Caucasian Army's mainstays during the early months of the war was the locally recruited frontier guards. These men knew the land, the local languages and how to fight following decades of running battles with smugglers. What they lacked in style they more than made up for in enterprise and initiative. Their role became that of scouts and partisans when the number of infantry increased and released them from mundane duties.

A fearsome group of Caucasian Cossack scouts undergo machine-gun training with an instructor wearing the St George's Cross. Thousands of Cossacks from the Kuban and Terek hosts fought on this front. Significant numbers operated on foot in *plastuni* battalions as well as on horseback. Their traditional dress, as seen here, was also worn into action.

Turkish POWs, bedraggled, frostbitten and starving, await transport to the rear after the invasion of 1914–15 ends in disaster.

Captured Turkish guns at Sarikamish. As the pack and draught animals died or were eaten, guns were simply abandoned during the Turkish retreat.

A Russian 76mm Putilov field gun in position somewhere in Anatolia. The shell cases were kept safe for recycling as ammunition was in short supply.

To overcome his supply difficulties Yudenitch employed thousands of camels as baggage animals. A convoy of such is seen here wending its way along a so-called main road. Providing supplies for the supply columns led to the creation of dozens of staging posts, always sited at a source of fresh water.

Cossack scouts report back to a senior intelligence officer in the Anatolian highlands. Time and again such men proved their worth as the maps of the area were not up to date. A useful source of information was the local Christian population which sympathised with the Russians.

General Yudenitch, fourth from left, his staff and bodyguard survey Turkish positions. Yudenitch enjoyed a good reputation with his men as he was sparing of their lives and kept a close eye on their welfare and health. He was respected by the Grand Duke Nicholas who used his influence to increase the quota of supplies allocated to this front.

A Schneider-Danglis M1909 76mm mountain gun at full recoil. It broke down into seven mule loads or could be towed where possible. With an elevation of 60 degrees, a range of 6,000m and a 6kg shell it was an excellent weapon for the terrain.

The evacuation of casualties was a precarious task in this barren landscape. Horses were preferred by the wounded as they did not sway as much as camels.

Horses aboard the transport ship *Rivn* on the Black Sea sail towards Trebizond, summer 1916. As well as supporting sea-borne assaults, such vessels were used to supply forward positions as it was simpler to use the water than the land routes. Cattle transport boats known as *elpidiphores* were used as landing craft as the bow of the boat dropped in a way that enabled infantry to dismount into the surf.

Captured Turkish flags at Trebizond are proudly displayed for the camera. Images of such trophies played well to the public starved of success in the West.

On 4 August 1916 the Grand Duke Nicholas reviewed an unusual British unit that had just arrived in Tiflis from Murmansk – the Russian Armoured Car Division Royal Naval Air Service, under the leadership of Commander Oliver Locker-Lampson MP.

The three squadrons of British armoured cars were split up, with one going to northern Persia, the others to operate near Mus. The Russians were somewhat at loss as to what to do with this Allied aid and did not interfere. The vehicles seen here are Lanchesters of No. 3 Squadron. The unit was supported by a wide variety of maintenance and other machines.

The Royal Navy's armoured car force in Anatolia crosses a dry stream bed. After several months of patrolling and combat with both Turkish regulars and Kurdish irregulars it was transferred to the Romanian Front during the autumn of 1916. The Grand Duke felt there would be more scope for these vehicles in that area.

Just behind the front line Russian troops brew up with stones acting as a windbreak. Daily rations were plain but sustaining. Tea was unlimited; the meat ration was 0.45kg; bread 0.9kg; and sugar 0.25kg.

Armenian refugees pose for the Russian press. The full extent of the suffering endured by the Christian population of eastern Anatolia at the hands of the Turks and their allies or the Moslems at the hands of the invaders is unlikely ever to be truly calculated. It is interesting to note the lack of men who were recruited into Russian-sponsored units.

Cossacks of Baratov's command ride into Persia. In November 1916 co-operation with the British advance in Persia was deemed sensible and Baratov was allocated a large force of Georgian and Armenian infantry to facilitate this. However, the March Revolution brought an end to this planned joint action as operations in this theatre wound down.

Chapter Five

An Area Bigger Than Belgium

The shorter line stabilised following the Great Retreat, which coincided with the Tsar's assumption of the mantle of Supreme Commander-in-Chief and the organisation of the three fronts. Following this, SW Front, under the command of General N.I. Ivanov, prepared to launch a winter offensive against the Austrians in the Bukovina area near the Romanian border. It was the conquest of Serbia that presented Stavka with the opportunity to attack what was perceived to be a weakened Austrian position. Seventh and Ninth armies were expected to drive the Austrians back to the Carpathians after their artillery had ploughed their defences to nothing.

In many respects the Russian tactics were to be a copy of those employed by Mackensen at Gorlice–Tarnow – deploy sufficient guns on a narrow front and simply blow the enemy away. Unfortunately, the Russian gunners did not locate their opposite numbers and the snow itself masked much of the effectiveness of the explosives. Inevitably, very little of the wire was cut. After a 36-hour bombardment the infantry attacked on 28 December. The first line of Austrian trenches was taken but then the attack bogged down. Supporting troops had to march up to 3km to reach the front line and presented clear targets for the enemy artillery, which was supported by aerial observers. In some places no-man's-land was up to 1km wide, the crossing of which could take a laden man in the snow several minutes – long enough for a machine-gunner to take position. Well provided with men and ammunition, the attacks continued for ten days. Finally, at the cost of 50,000 casualties, the Russians had begun to learn that more artillery does not lead inevitably to victory. Tragically, this lesson would have to be repeated three months later on the N Front.

The failure of SW Front's offensive led Ivanov to report to Stavka that his command was in no condition to mount further attacks. Indeed, such was his lack of faith in his men that he ordered the defences of Kiev be strengthened against the possibility of an Austrian breakthrough. Such behaviour obviously came to the notice of Stavka and Alexeyev began moves to have Ivanov replaced.

Despite SW Front's failure, as 1916 dawned Stavka was in an optimistic mood. The morale of the men was improving, as noted by the military postal censors, units were filling up with replacements and domestic munitions supplies were now overtaking wastage and even demand. The appointment of Polivanov and the work of the supply committees had begun to bear fruit.

At the Chantilly conference Russia had agreed to carry out an offensive during the summer simultaneously with Britain and France. Alexeyev, however, had anticipated an earlier German attack in the West, and when the Verdun offensive began on 21 February 1916 his premonition became grim reality. So too did the French request for a Russian attack to relieve the pressure on Verdun. General N.A. Kuropatkin's N Front and W Front, led by General A.E. Evert, were ordered to attack the German lines jointly near Lake Narotch. Men and guns moved into position, particularly behind W Front's Second Army on which the responsibility for the main attack would fall. It was to form the southern flank of a pincer movement linking up with N Front's Fifth Army. The build-up behind Russian lines did not go unnoticed by the Germans as reports from their airmen were confirmed by wireless intercepts. The Russians' target was obvious and defences strengthened as a consequence.

The attack zone was some 97km wide, of which almost one-third was marshland or lake which was frozen at this time of the year. With 350,000 men backed by 1,000 guns both front commanders felt quietly confident despite the replacement of Second Army's commander with General A.F. Ragoza (who knew nothing of the area) at the last moment.

Preceded by an 80-minute barrage, the attack started at 1020hr on 18 March. Assaulting on a 2km-wide front over ground that rapidly and most unseasonably churned into mud and water up to ½m in depth, the attack bogged down. Incredibly, the Russian infantry penetrated the German lines to a depth of 2km across a ½km frontage. That night the frost returned. Fifth Army achieved a similar penetration. The mixed weather continued but with the temperature steadily rising towards the end of March fog blanketed much of the marshy battlefield, turning it into a place of surreal nightmare. By the end of April the operation was called off. Up to 100,000 Russian casualties, 5 times those of the Germans, had bought a sliver of mud that was retaken several weeks later. However, such was the scale of the disaster that an enquiry was launched which gathered much useful information. For War Minister Polivanov such data was academic as the Tsar dismissed him on 28 March for becoming too close to politicians and non-government agencies. But for General A.A. Brusilov, commander of Eighth Army on SW Front since 1914, it made positive good sense.

Despite Alexeyev's doubts, Brusilov was, on 30 March, promoted to the command of SW Front. Ivanov, broken in spirit, was present at Stavka in mid-April when it was decided to launch the major Russian summer offensive north of the Pripet Marshes utilising N and W Fronts.

Both Evert and Kuropatkin reacted negatively to this proposition. Declaring the German lines to be impregnable, they both claimed a lack of heavy artillery as the cause of their inevitable failure. However, reassurances were given along with a promise of heavy guns. Consequently, Evert grudgingly agreed to launch an offensive along a 20km front with the support of 1,000 guns, a 2-month period for preparation and help from N Front. At this point Brusilov weighed in with the offer of a localised attack that would require no more forces than he already had. His offer was accepted. When the conference ended on 14 April the three front commanders returned to their HQs with varying degrees of confidence. Brusilov immediately gathered his army commanders and outlined his plans for a series of diversionary attacks along the entirety of SW Front, where they faced a wholly Austrian series of armies.

Brusilov intended to use tactical innovation rather than weight of shell to break through what was a formidable defensive line. The Austrians, having shifted their attention to the Italian Front, had dug three defensive lines from south of the Pripet Marshes almost to the Romanian border. Heavily wired no-man's-land varied in depth from 100m to over 1km before well-sited, concrete machine-gun positions and deep, solidly built trenches were encountered. Brusilov's subordinates were ordered to train their men on replicas of Austrian defence works and make use of specially trained grenadier platoons to infiltrate them. However, as the Russian build-up proceeded, the Italians appealed for help as they were under pressure from a major Austrian offensive. Alexeyev had no wish to begin his offensive prematurely but caved in to pressure from the Tsar. Evert argued that he would be unable to attack until mid-June but Brusilov stated that he was ready to go and the diversionary attacks promised by SW Front began on 4 June 1916.

Along the length of SW Front the Russians pushed forward. After just over a week's fighting more than 200 guns and 100,000 POWs were in Russian hands. The Austrian line was collapsing as Russian cavalry raided up to 30km behind their trenches. The Austrian offensive in Italy was cancelled and German troops were rushed eastwards, including four divisions from the Verdun area. Despite this obvious success, Evert yet again postponed his attack and Kuropatkin remained equally passive. Finally, during the first week of July, when the British were being slaughtered on the Somme, Evert and Kuropatkin moved. However, by mid-July both front's attacks had petered out with little to show for 80,000 casualties.

With this failure the Tsar's faith in Evert declined and Alexeyev, taking full advantage of the situation, gifted Brusilov Third Army and the elite of Russia's land forces, the Guards Army. With these two fresh formations Brusilov was to attack

Kovel and put the entire German line northwards to the Baltic coast in jeopardy. Brusilov explained the operation to a British observer thus, 'Third Army was to attack Kovel to the west, Guards Army to the north-west and Eighth Army to the south and on to Vladimir Volinsk. Eleventh Army was to move towards Lemberg and then wheel north, its left supported by Seventh Army. Ninth Army would get its turn when Romania joins in.'

On 28 July Guards Army attacked and pushed back the newly arrived German reinforcements to the Stokhod River. Unfortunately, the battleground now included large areas of marsh land narrowing the attack lanes to stretches of dry ground which provided wonderful killing zones for machine guns and aircraft. The Guards were cut to pieces, suffering 30,000 casualties by the end of the first week in August. Out of the line since December 1914, the Guards had not been trained for or exposed to the current methods of fighting and its leadership was poor in the extreme. Brusilov expressed his rage and discontent with the Guards' commanders in a letter to Alexeyev but nothing was done as senior officers in the Guards were royal appointees. Eventually, the losses sickened the Tsar himself who removed the Guard's commander and replaced him with General V.I. Gurko. The Guards Army was renamed the Special Army and as such was returned to the W Front along with Third Army. However, this did not halt the slaughter at Kovel where the Central Powers gradually increased the strength of the defences. N Front, quiet but for some feeble demonstrations before Riga, witnessed the arrival of a new commander, General N.V. Ruzski. Kuropatkin was sent to Turkestan to deal with an uprising of the Moslem population, a job better suited to his limited abilities.

The return of Third and Special armies to W Front effectively ended what became known as the Brusilov Offensive. Nevertheless, SW Front's advance continued and its leading elements reached the foothills of the Carpathian Mountains by mid-September, although the recapture of Lemberg eluded it. By this time Brusilov's dwindling forces had reached the limit of what they could achieve without a long respite to build up their supply lines and bring in replacements. Looking at a map, the achievements of SW Front were spectacular – 25,000km^2 of territory, almost the land mass of Belgium, had been taken by mid-October when the fighting ceased.

Brusilov ordered his army commanders to occupy the most advantageous ground within 100m of the enemy. Nor were they to cease hostilities completely. Raiding was to be actively encouraged as training for the newly arrived conscripts throughout the autumn and winter. Officers were to 'from time to time provoke close fighting in trenches especially using trench mortars instead of artillery, hand grenades instead of bayonets. These districts also had to act as fighting schools for divisions and corps.'

Totalling up SW Front's achievements beyond the territory gained, the statistics were remarkable – 400,000 POWs, nearly 1,800 machines guns and almost 600 guns were captured. For the sake of convenience entire Russian units were armed with Austrian rifles, such were the mountains of ammunition captured. The towns of Halicz and Brody in the Bukovina had fallen and the province cleared of enemy forces. The crushing defeat of the Austrians south of the Pripet Marshes effectively ended their control of their military destiny on the Eastern Front. German staff officers were scattered throughout the Austrian command structure as men of Russia's Ninth Army eyed the Carpathian passes in eager anticipation of further glory.

But it was not only the Russians that the Hapsburg Empire had to fear, for as almost a direct result of SW Front's efforts during June–August Romania had finally declared herself to be a part of the Allied coalition and invaded Transylvania.

One of the older conscripts, the so-called *borodachi* (bearded ones), called up during 1915. The mobilisation orders of that year caused widespread unrest as they deprived families of their breadwinners. There were frequent instances of fighting with the police and in the more remote areas gangs of conscription dodgers hid out in the forests living like bandits.

In September 1915 Ivanov had recorded that 'the number of soldiers travelling without documents on the railways is increasing'. The Tsar responded by increasing the level of surveillance of roads and railway stations to reduce desertion.

Generals Evert and Kuropatkin at Stavka, early 1916. Neither man wished to risk his reputation on an offensive that year. Their fear of fighting the Germans was such that they were rendered impotent and regarded such aggressive leaders as Brusilov almost insane.

Representatives at the Allied conference at Chantilly pausing for a photo call. The conference concluded that mutual support would be provided in the event of a serious enemy attack. The assault on Verdun fell into this category and Russia was duty bound to respond.

Troops for weapons – men of Russia's First Special Brigade disembark at Marseilles, April 1916. Despite Alexeyev's objections, the Tsar had sanctioned what was effectively a swap of men for munitions several months before. Alexeyev was quoted as saying, 'we are so dependent on the French for war materiel that the categorical refusal we should give is out of the question'.

On 30 December 1914 the Tsar presented medals to men of the Guard Rifles at Novo Minsk railway station in Poland. On 22 June 1915 the Guard was withdrawn from the front to refit, expand and train. Its commander, General V.M. Bezobrazov, was replaced only to be reinstated by the Tsar months later on 19 October, much to Alexeyev's disgust.

An officer displays a collection of weapons. The rifle is a Japanese Arisaka, one of thousands imported to make up the shortfall in production. Issued primarily to naval units to ease ammunition supply problems, they found their way to the front line along with the bayonet seen. The grenades cover almost every type, both hand and rifle-powered, employed by the Russians.

A younger recruit called up during 1915. His equipment is mainly canvas due to the shortage of leather. The chest bandolier is designed for cartridge clips. The standard-issue Mosin-Nagant rifle took a five-round clip. The belt buckle is a simpler version of that issued to officers and cheaper to make than the original enlisted man's belt plate. Such new men were often referred to as *Polivantsy* after the Minister of War.

The mud-soaked attacks at Lake Narotch were a proving ground for some of the new conscripts. Here they would learn the reality of modern winter warfare. Squatting in the filth, many of the new men must have wondered where this France they were helping was.

Inside a captured German trench Russian soldiers guard a trophy of war – a spring-powered trench mortar plus some grenades. Captured weapons such as this were usually put to use against their former owners. The shallowness of the trench is a result of the local water table.

Having experienced the effects of gas warfare, the Russians had begun to develop their own masks. Here new recruits practice musketry in their protective gear. Various types were produced and underwent extensive front-line trials before a final version was adopted.

One of Brusilov's innovations was to direct his men to tunnel underneath enemy wire, and here the entrance to such a tunnel can be seen. Earth was removed under cover of darkness. The tunnels sloped upwards and were only breached when the attack took place. The observers are measuring the distance to open ground from the cover of metal shields.

SW Front also deployed considerable numbers of aircraft to spot for the artillery prior to the offensive. The majority were luckier than the crew of this Voisin III. This aircraft, imported in large numbers from France, was also built under licence in Moscow.

To prevent enemy observation of reserves Brusilov ordered the construction of immense dugouts, capable of holding several thousand men, close to the front lines where men could wait in relative comfort and safety until it was their turn to join the attackers. What conditions were like in such cramped conditions is best left to the imagination however unconcerned these officers appear.

A shattered Austrian armoured train (possibly number 7) is inspected by a Russian officer. Several armoured trains were sent to provide the Austrians with mobile artillery. This unit operated in support of Second Army. It has clearly been comprehensively destroyed by artillery fire to its forward gun wagon.

German POWs are marched to the rear by men of SW Front. The bulk of them would be shipped to Turkestan or Siberia where food was more readily available and escape well-nigh impossible. The Tsaritsa's humanitarian, charitable attitude to these men was further evidence of her pro-German sympathies for those who were intent on blackening her name.

Brusilov's artillery fire plan was designed with intervals of several minutes in built. The purpose of these was to encourage the defenders into the belief that the attack was imminent so they would leave their bunkers and man the fire steps. The barrage would then resume and send them back underground. After several such episodes the Austrians would become reluctant to come out. This time lapse enabled the Russians to get close to or even into the trenches before their opponents were ready to fight. It was a remarkably effective tactic which netted hundreds of POWS with hardly a shot fired.

Russian officers relax in the Austrian front line. The solidity of the defences is evident. However, many of these 'miniature Przemysls', as the Austrian bunkers were nicknamed, proved to be too effective and the men in them reluctant to venture out.

The price of victory. Russian dead near the lip of the Austrian third line of trenches await burial. The portable wire defences have been moved to the rear to stop counterattacks. In the distance can be seen the foothills of the Carpathian Mountains.

Chapter Six

The Romanian Ulcer

Until the outbreak of war in 1914 Romania had been secretly allied to Germany and Austria for reasons of family – the Romanian royal family was closely related to Germany's ruling house – and strategy – Romania resented Russia's snatching of Bessarabia as a reward for helping her gain independence from the Turks in 1878. However, the Hapsburg province of Transylvania was also eyed jealously from Bucharest. Therefore, reneging on the treaty made Romania something of an untrustworthy outcast in the eyes of the Central Powers. Simply put, from 1914 to mid-1916 Romania's government had made considerable political, diplomatic and financial capital from both sides as they vied for her support. The largest oil field accessible to the Central Powers was at Ploesti in Romania and her bountiful harvests were also vital, particularly for Austria's food needs. Therefore, food and raw materials had been supplied to both Germany and Austria for exceedingly high prices from the outset. In October 1914 Russia's Foreign Minister had, in order to secure the Black Sea coast and Ukraine from invasion, agreed that Romania should receive Transylvania in return for 'benevolent neutrality'.

Romania's border to the south with Bulgaria was defined by the mighty Danube River as far as Silistria then across land to the Black Sea. From this point, just south of Varna to the Danube delta, was the former Bulgarian province of Dobrudja which Bulgaria dearly wished to regain. To the west Romania's Austrian border ran along the Carpathian Mountains and to the north and east its border with Russia followed the Pruth River.

Entente negotiations with Romania had been ongoing since the outbreak of war but stepped up rapidly in 1916, particularly as SW Front appeared to be on the point of destroying Austria's capacity to continue fighting. Consequently, Romania did not wish to miss the chance of a place at any peace negotiations. However, her entry into the war was dependent on three conditions. A Russian force of 50,000 men was to protect the Dobrudja against Bulgarian incursion, 300 tons of munitions were to be supplied daily and energetic action by the Russians coupled with an Allied attack on the Salonika Front was to divert forces to that area. With agreement reached, much to Alexeyev's chagrin, Romania declared war on Austria and moved troops through the Carpathian passes into Transylvania beginning on 28 August. The Central Powers were taken by surprise, not expecting an assault until late September when the Romanian harvest would have been gathered in.

A plodding advance by First and Second Romanian armies gained the city of Kronstadt but also signalled the high-water mark of the offensive. Fourth Army, to the left of SW Front, maintained a tenuous link to Second Army on its left flank. The Romanians held these positions for several weeks allowing Falkenhayn to assemble a variety of units that included Germany's Alpine Corps and Austrian mountain troops, all of which were experienced specialists in mountain warfare. Alongside other Austro-German formations the whole comprised the Ninth Army which soon forced the Romanian First and Second armies onto the defensive. By early October the Ninth Army had pushed their opponents back through the mountains onto their own soil.

Russia's contribution consisted of 61st Infantry Division, 3rd Cavalry Division and the Serbian Division (raised from Austrian POWs and Serb volunteers) and only began to cross the Danube River into Dobrudja on 10 September as there was no bridge in the area. With Ninth Austro-German Army now debouching onto the plains of Romania the government in Bucharest appealed to Stavka for help. The Russian reply was blunt – withdraw to a defensible position running from the Black Sea port of Constanza, through Bucharest to the Predeal Pass where Fourth and Second Romanian armies connected. Such a move would have entailed the loss of a quarter of their lands and therefore the Romanians ignored this suggestion.

Following a surprise attack the Russo-Romanian forces in Dobrudja were driven back by an army of Turks, Bulgars and Germans led by the redoubtable General von Mackensen. By 20–1 October the Russo-Romanians had had both flanks turned and fell back pursued closely by Bulgarian cavalry. The great port of Constanza was evacuated and vast quantities of oil and grain were captured by Mackensen's troops. However, there was little love lost between the nationalities of his command and the advance to the Danube River slowed to a crawl, much to the German's frustration. Unfortunately, a similar lack of cohesion existed on the other side of the line. Russian contempt for their ally grew by the day, as did Romanian disgust for their erstwhile ally's general high-handedness.

As a result of losses incurred by mid-November, the Romanians had found it necessary to combine infantry divisions. As this process was underway on 16–17 November the Romanian defences east of the Carpathian Mountains cracked and German cavalry broke through creating chaos and panic in the rear areas.

Just over a week later, supported by gunboats of the Austrian Danube Flotilla, the Danube was crossed 100km south-west of Bucharest by elements of Mackensen's force. A counterattack, 'to throw him [Mackensen] into the Danube' failed, according to the Romanians, because of the lack of Russian assistance. 'They [the Russians] did not actually refuse but stalled [and] gave promises'. Neither Russian Seventh Army in the Bukovina nor the Army of the Dobrudja along the Danube moved and engaged in only minor skirmishes. Stavka's perceived intransigence provoked a direct appeal for reinforcements for the Bucharest defences to the Tsar himself. Nicholas agreed and an army corps began to move, slowly, in that direction. With its capital in peril and its army disintegrating, the Romanian government declared Bucharest an open city and on 6 December Mackensen accepted its surrender. On the same day Bavarian infantry occupied Ploesti, the centre of the oil fields. However, many of the wells and masses of the equipment had been destroyed by a team of British saboteurs which had received little help from the local authorities. So effective was their work that the sky was reported as being black for over 100km. The Romanian government relocated to Jassy near the Russian border where its army, now reduced to a mass of semi-refugees, reassembled as Stavka pumped in reinforcements and took over almost the entire front line. In December 1916 a new staff was created which was to be responsible for the Romanian Front under the command of General V.V. Sakharov. The Entente's Eastern Front now ran from the Baltic to the Black Sea. The reformation of the Romanian Army proceeded under the auspices of a French Military Mission led by General Berthelot, to which the Russians contributed 60,000 Austrian rifles. More supplies were to be forthcoming from the Western Allies via the north Russian ports, but the journey would be long and difficult and involve the laying of a new railway line into Romania. The intervention of Romania had proved a double-edged sword and was to be a mixed blessing to the Russians during the months to come. Luckily for Stavka, the weather proved savage enough to curtail any operations in Romania as the Central Powers divided up their considerable loot. Many Romanians questioned the wisdom of their government's actions of the summer as they shivered in the huge refugee camps that sprang up.

As winter came to the town of Mogilev, the location of Stavka, on the upper Dnieper River so too did a new Chief-of-Staff. Alexeyev had been taken seriously ill, so much so that he was temporarily replaced by General V.I. Gurko in November 1916.

Having established the new Romanian Front, Gurko received the news that it had been agreed at Chantilly that Russia would take the offensive in April 1917. This time it was to be the SW Front that would shoulder the main role. Brusilov was tasked with three objectives, the capture of Kovel and Lemberg and to provide support for the Romanians. Brusilov commented, 'This time my front [would be] given relatively considerable resources for use in the offensive.' Part of these 'considerable resources' was to be the ultra-secret XLVIII Army Corps under the command of

General G.M. Scheidemann. This corps came into being officially on 2 January 1917. Its title was Heavy Artillery of Special Purpose/Duty, more easily rendered by its Russian acronym of TAON. The theory underlying the TAON was simple – to organise an entire artillery corps of guns greater than 107mm to form what was essentially a battering ram, in Second World War Soviet terms a Breakthrough Artillery Corps. Consequently, its existence had to be kept secret because its deployment would point a direct finger at the target of the offensive. The TAON was to be made up of as much heavy artillery as could be wrested from the four front commanders, as well incorporating all imported British and French guns of suitable calibre and thus easing problems of shell supply by centralisation via the corps HQ at Smolensk. Reluctant as the front commanders were to part with their heavy artillery, they did so. As many of the hundreds of guns moving towards the assembly points were semi-mobile, it was decided that the TAON would have an almost entirely motorised transport and supply column with an integral aerial observation unit of fifteen balloons. By early February 300 guns had arrived and distribution into the 6 brigades, numbered 200–5, that made up the corps began.

Reform of the infantry and cavalry was also in hand as January 1917 began. The number of infantry divisions was to be expanded by a reduction and redistribution of the battalions in the existing divisions. From sixteen the number of battalions would be cut to twelve, with the surplus being used to create new divisions. The new divisions would be attached to existing army corps, thus expanding them to three-division formations. New artillery units were to be created by a ruthless assessment of local needs. Areas perceived to be relatively quiet would lose their modern guns, which would be replaced by older, less-mobile weapons. The final reform involved the cavalry, each division of which would now dismount sufficient men to provide 2,000 infantrymen for use as such in each division. The spare horses would be deployed to draw the eight 114mm howitzers (British imported 4.5in pieces) that each cavalry division would receive.

Unfortunately, many senior officers viewed this reorganisation as an opportunity to dispose of its older, less-experienced men – the over 40s – who had been called up during 1915. Thousands of these troops were moved into the third divisions which rapidly became breeding grounds for disaffection and demoralisation. As all of these facets of change fell into place, planning began for the summer offensive, but preparations for two other operations were also in train at the extremes of the front. To the south Vice Admiral A.V. Kolchak, commander of the Black Sea Fleet since July 1916, had been given responsibility for organising an amphibious attack on Constantinople. The first stage of this was to assemble a large number of transport vessels, including barges from the redundant Romanian Danube River Fleet, and from the Caucasian ports. Naval cover increased dramatically when, on 30

November 1916, the Black Sea Fleet launched its first dreadnought, which was the most powerful warship in those waters. An infantry division, of four regiments, was placed at Kolchak's disposal by the Tsar on 24 December. It was entitled the Black Sea Division and its first regiment was named Constantinople (*Tsargradski* in Russian), while the others were named after defenders of Sevastopol during the Crimean War. These men were to be the first landed on Turkish soil near the Ottoman capital. The Turco-German naval threat on the Black Sea had been much reduced by the loss of three U-boats and the laying up of the *Goeben* and the *Breslau* for long-term repairs. The time frame for the launching of Operation Bosporus was mid-June to mid-August 1917 and depended on Stavka releasing a further two divisions of infantry.

The second operation's location lay in less balmy climes on the Baltic Sea coast near Riga. During the autumn of 1916 eight Latvian infantry regiments had been brigaded with II and VI Siberian army corps. This concentration of some 30,000 Latvians had one purpose, to drive the Germans from Courland. What became known as the 'Christmas Battle' began at 0500hr on 5 January 1917. As the snow fell, sappers, dressed in white camouflage gear, cut or bridged the wire with mats and very quickly the first line of German trenches were captured. However, the advance ground to a halt in front of a position named, for obvious reasons, Machine Gun Hill, which was taken after three days at the cost of heavy casualties. Unfortunately, support from the Siberians was not forthcoming. Fighting dragged on until the end of January for no appreciable gains. Indeed, the attitude displayed by the Russians fostered a deep sense of mistrust among the Latvians who felt their heavy losses had been for nought.

The discontent felt by the Latvians was not the only murmur of unrest in the Tsar's empire, however. In Petrograd members of the Duma were becoming increasingly outspoken regarding the conduct of domestic policy. Then, in the early hours of 30 December the Tsaritsa's *éminence grise*, Rasputin, was murdered by a group of courtiers close to the royal family. The news reached the Tsar at Stavka during a front commanders' conference over which he was presiding, displaying his usual obvious boredom. Brusilov remembered, 'on hearing the news [he] hurriedly bade us farewell and left us'. Nicholas was not to return to his HQ until 7 March, by which time his world was beginning to spin out of control.

A Russian machine gun under well-prepared cover.

The Romanian railway system was of the standard European gauge which differed from the Russian. Here Russian railway troops prepare a platform by a newly laid spur line. At the Russian border the wagons were moved by crane onto the appropriate set of wheels for the lines on which they would be travelling. Consequently, a bottleneck built up at the changeover point.

The Russian armed forces took the spiritual welfare of the men very seriously. This seaborne church was used by the Black Sea Fleet. Similar small-scale buildings were mounted on railway flatcars.

Russian wounded are evacuated by what appear to be FIAT lorries of the RNACD, which was posted to the Romanian Front in late 1916.

The front line in Romania was a microcosm of the conditions elsewhere in the East. From the Black Sea coast the flat land rose steadily until it reached the foothills of the Carpathian Mountains. Here Russians look out from an oddly straight trench line which appears to have seen little fighting.

However, when the winter of 1916–17 came the men were often unable to dig in and were forced to fight from the cover of rapidly improvised barricades.

A Russian cavalry regiment's band rides into a Romanian town, autumn 1916.

In November 1916 the railway line from Murmansk to Petrozavodsk, which then ran on to Petrograd, was opened. It had been built by German and Austrian POWs when local labour was not forthcoming. It has been suggested that up 20,000 POWs died while carrying out this work. Indentured Chinese labour completed the line.

Bulgarian troops played an important part in the Romanian campaign. Romania had not expected their participation because Bulgaria owed its independence to Russia. They were sadly mistaken as Bulgaria's desire to regain the Dobrudja region was of paramount importance.

The light Russian mountain gun was deployed in considerable numbers in the low Carpathian foothills. Although the Russians had no specialist mountain troops, as the Austrians and Germans did, they did have excellent artillery for these areas.

A medal presentation ceremony on the Romanian Front, early 1917.

A Russian trench mortar section, early 1917. For the Romanians the art and weaponry of trench warfare were new topics that they would learn at considerable cost once the front settled into positional warfare.

Nieuport XIs lined up, spring 1917. The Romanian air force was microscopic and its experience nil. Consequently, the Russians were obliged to provide air support for the front. On the upper wing is the stripped down air combat version of the Lewis gun.

By late 1916 the Tsaritsa and her daughters had involved themselves in nursing and charity work. These men are pictured eating in a hospital dining room having been served by members of the royal family who are not in shot. The wounds are all above the waistline.

Nor was the Tsar's mother tardy with her good works. This hospital is sponsored by the Dowager Empress, who is pictured to the Tsar's left along with medical staff and her retinue.

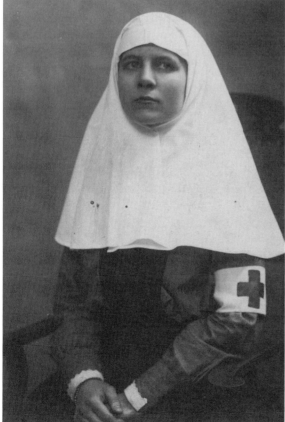

Russia's wealthier citizens sponsored entire hospital trains and the daughters of those who could not provide so generously often volunteered for nursing work. However, there were those who complained that the hospital trains of some aristocrats seemed to serve exclusively to the rear of guard divisions. Nevertheless, nurses proved themselves time and again by following the attack waves to serve the wounded. Russia was one of the first countries to encourage female doctors.

Once the Romanians had learned the lessons of modern warfare and reorganised their forces they fought the Austro-German summer counter-offensive to a standstill at the battles of Marashti and Marasheshti. However, from September 1917 they were reduced to holding the line and waiting on events. This Romanian officer was photographed in 1916.

On 7 December Romania signed an armistice with the Central Powers. However, their negotiators strung the treat talks out until 7 May 1918. With the collapse of the Central Powers in November that year Romania remobilised and re-entered the war just in time to take a place at the peace talks, which saw her gain both Transylvania and Bessarabia. Here Russian troops prepare to take up positions following the armistice.

Chapter Seven

Trench Warfare on the Eastern Front

The fighting on the European sector of the Russian Front was in many ways similar to that on the Western Front – men dug in and waited for the 'Big Push', the offensive that would overwhelm their enemies and end the war. However, in the east the lines were longer, the men fewer and the nature of the terrain dictated a different way of waging war. Prior to the retreat from Poland the length of the front from the Baltic coast to the Romanian border was some 1,700km but with the conclusion of the Austro-German advance during the summer of 1915 it was reduced to a little over 1,000km. The Brusilov Offensive added depth but relatively little length to the front. However, the intervention and subsequent collapse of Romania in 1916 extended this line by some 350km. Running from the coast of the Baltic to the Black Sea, the front passed through a varied selection of ground cut by rivers, ground often over 300m and the vast watery, wilderness of the Pripet Marshes which took up roughly 75km of the line where SW and W Fronts met. Nevertheless, in places the trench system became quite highly developed, while in others it was almost non-existent due to the wet conditions. Much of the soil was very sandy which, when wet, turned to glutinous mud. Furthermore, along considerable stretches of the front the gap between friend and foe was up to a kilometre or more. Large, dark almost primeval forest stretched north and south of the Pripet Marshes and down into Romania. Consequently, there were significant areas that were covered by infantry or cavalry screens supported by a few guns and local militia. As both the Brusilov and Mackensen offensives had demonstrated, it was easy enough to break through but increasingly difficult to maintain momentum because of the lack of infrastructure and the consequent inevitable breakdown of the supply chain due to the distances involved.

As the Central Powers had determined to undertake no major operations in the East following the failure of the Black-Yellow Offensive during the autumn of 1915, preferring to concentrate their efforts elsewhere, they had dug in where possible. This was not the case for Stavka. Following the lull after the Russians fell back from the Polish salient in 1915, they had been considering their options regarding assault and trench-fighting tactics. Independently, various infantry and cavalry formations had been grouping their scouting platoons into larger units and using them for aggressive activities such as trench raids and reconnaissance. As the Austrian staff noted, 'where the distance between the lines was very great, a battle for possession of "no man's land" ensued . . . [our] *jagdkommandos* [hunting commandos] were modelled on their Russian counterparts . . .'. Russia's XXV Corps, part of Western Front, took this tactic further during October 1915. The fourth platoon in every company was to be transformed into a grenadier platoon. Picked from 'brave and energetic men', they were to be armed with ten grenades, a shovel, an axe and wire cutters. These weapons were rapidly supplemented with carbines, revolvers, short lances and broadswords. The grenadiers were to carry out trench raids but more particularly to lead attacks in conjunction with the sappers by preparing the way, destroying obstacles such as wire and bunkers, with specialist explosives. When the training period ended in December 1915 it was decided that all regiments, other than the Guards, on all fronts should assemble grenadier platoons of 'one officer, four NCOs and 48 men'. By early 1917 the practice was widespread and generally successful, and therefore it was decided that these assault platoons should be expanded into battalions with integral trench artillery, signallers and machine-gun sections.

The structure of a 'Shock' battalion (often referred to as Death battalions), one for each regiment, was outlined in order number 320/48 to the Special Army in early 1917. Each battalion was to consist of three rifle companies and a technical section which would include the elements noted previously. The machine-gun section included eight light weapons, such as the Lewis or the French Chauchat, as well as eight heavier Maxims. One grenade that was specified was the Novikov, complete with string attachments for entangling, specifically designed to destroy wire entanglements. The combat instructions for these units noted that they were to fight, 'exclusively in the trenches, so-called open battle, on the surface of the earth was seen as the exception'. Ideally, training for specific attacks was undertaken on replicas of the trench and defensive obstacles modelled from aerial photos, ground observation and first-hand reconnaissance. The latter was particularly emphasised, as was the use of camouflage and surprise. No mention was made of transferring men into these formations from other parts of a higher unit. However, it is unlikely that men of the calibre noted above would be released by their commanders as it would dilute the effectiveness of their original unit. This became particularly important when the reliability of the men began to decline following the March Revolution. The need to assemble units of reliable, well-motivated soldiers rapidly became an issue that Brusilov (as commander of SW Front) chose to address during May 1917. At that time, the Delegation of the Black Sea, formed from soldiers, sailors and civilians from the Black Sea ports and defences, with the support of Admiral Kolchak, visited Moscow, Petrograd and the Baltic Sea bases. They were calling for the restoration of discipline and the continuation of the war and were joined by a group of sympathisers from SW Front. The delegates, through Brusilov, called for the formation of special 'Shock, revolutionary, battalions recruited from volunteers' drawn from the rear.

Kerensky was agreeable as this corresponded with his ideas of democratising the army but Alexeyev had reservations which became irrelevant when he was replaced as Supreme Commander-in-Chief by Brusilov shortly after. Such formations as came into being drew from a weird and wonderful variety of recruitment pools, ranging from disillusioned troops who wanted to continue the war to a victorious conclusion to idealistic adolescents from the towns and cities far behind the lines to those who simply joined up for the preferential rates of pay, pension and the cachet such units attracted. Some, like the 1st Shock Detachment, were serious, committed soldiers, others were little but specially badged (chevrons and other insignia distinguished these troops) formations of shirkers. Their training was to have been similar to that of the regular Shock troops as noted above, but frequently fell far short of those standards. Nevertheless, those battalions that reached the front often acquitted themselves bravely during the Kerensky Offensive and usually remained loyal to the Provisional Government until the demobilisation of the army. Several of the Shock battalions were involved in fighting pro-Bolshevik troops near Stavka and elesewhere behind the lines during the weeks following the November Revolution.

Specialist infantry formations were not the only method that the Russians employed to break the stalemate of trench warfare. Alongside their allies, the Russians also seriously considered the use of armoured vehicles. During Brusilov's push towards Lutsk during the summer of 1916 armoured cars had been used to support infantry attacks but were poorly co-ordinated and achieved little. There had been various Russian attempts to develop vehicles to break through trench systems that had come to nothing more than prototypes. However, the British and French development of tracked armoured vehicles, tanks, was watched with interest as had been their deployment in combat during 1916. Indeed, Brusilov remarked in his memoirs that during 1917 he looked forward to some being supplied to Russia, but he was to be disappointed. During the Petrograd conference of January 1917 the French agreed to provide some unspecified tanks but none were supplied.

During 1915 partisan units were formed, mainly from Cossack regiments, for the sole purpose of raiding behind enemy lines, where they were expected to gather POWs, intelligence and carry out acts of sabotage. Recollections of these units are mixed, some claim they caused more trouble than they were worth, others the reverse. Most were disbanded during 1916.

Gas and flamethrower weapons, fixed and portable, were under the control of the Chemical Battalion, established in late 1915 as a sub-branch of the artillery. The portable flamethrower sections, twelve weapons per section, were to be deployed in the front line as part of the trench-gun units under the 1917 reforms. The three-man flamethrower crews were to be trained as grenadiers and armed in a similar manner. However, the post-abdication confusion prevented this from being fully implemented. The base and training school for these specialists was Petrograd and following the crisis of July 1917 this establishment was disarmed and its men confined to barracks because of their Bolshevik sympathies. Interestingly, one of the most loyal units during these difficult few days was named the Voluntary Detachment of Crippled Warriors. Two battalions of the partially sighted, deaf and even limbless were formed from volunteers, many of whom were soldiers who had been invalided out, while others were disabled civilians previously exempted from service. The first battalion served on the W Front, the second took part in the suppression of the July uprising and members of the embryonic third were among the garrison of the Winter Palace when it was occupied during the November Revolution.

Grenadiers of an unidentified grenadier platoon pose for the camera, autumn 1916. Such was the secrecy attached to these formations that they were only issued with specialist badges in 1917. At least two men would carry steel shields.

The use of gas on the Eastern Front was less frequent than in the West. Here men trained by the Chemical Battalion prepare gas cylinders for storage underground. The Chemical Battalion trained personnel in the use of gas shells and static projectors and flamethrowers as well as testing and producing gas masks.

A group of Shkuro's 'Wolves', a partisan unit formed during the winter of 1915–16 from 3rd Khopersky Kuban Cossack Regiment and known officially as the Kuban Special Mounted Force. Commanded by Captain A.G. Shkuro, they carried out several successful raids behind German lines during 1916. The unit was transferred from the W to the SW Front later that year.

The weapon in the foreground is a 90mm heavy trench mortar mounted on solid wooden wheels to facilitate movement over muddy ground without the clogging associated with spokes. However, combined with the weight of the wooden base it proved difficult to manoeuvre. The Austrians noted Russian use of such weapons in 1914.

The Rosenberg 37mm Model 1915 went into service in early 1916. It was 50kg lighter than the Hotchkiss and broke into three parts. Easy to move in the confines of a trench, it was robust and accurate to 1,500m and its rate of fire was fifteen shots per minute. More than 200 were in front-line service by 1917.

The original Russian trench gun was the Hotchkiss 47mm, dating from the 1880s. Commandeered from surplus naval stock, they proved very useful. Firing only high-explosive shells to a range of 5,000m, its purpose was to knock out enemy machine-gun nests or strongpoints and to accompany infantry attacks. However, they were difficult to move due to their weight, 236kg, and size. Therefore, Stavka cast about for a smaller weapon; the result was the Rosenberg 37mm.

During late 1916 the haphazard organisation of trench artillery was rationalised. The Rosenberg and Hotchkiss guns were placed in eight gun batteries, distributed usually in pairs where required and attached to artillery brigades for supply purposes. From left to right, a Rosenberg-Maclean, similar to the original Rosenberg but with a different mount, a 90mm mortar, a Rosenberg and a 47mm mortar with projectile.

The upgrading of grenadier platoons to battalion-sized units coincided with the Revolution of March 1917 and the subsequent deterioration in officers' authority. Many officers chose to join the new formations. Here one such volunteer, in black staff officer's uniform, shows off a Winchester rifle. Imported from the USA, their rapid rate of fire and size was ideal for trench fighting. Swords were usually replaced with a shorter edged weapon.

An Aasen mortar, imported from France from 1915 onwards. Its calibre was 75mm and its range 400m. The weight, 25kg, made it easily man-portable over rough terrain and an ideal close-support weapon during attacks. Here one is being fired from concealment.

The Tsar, bearded and centre in uniform, accompanied by his Chief-of-Staff and members of Stavka watches a flamethrower demonstration, early May 1916. Part of the Chemical Battalion flamethrower detachments were allocated one to each of the thirteen armies at the front. This appears to be a Tovornitsky model crewed by three men. A static flamethrower, the SBS, was deployed in batteries of twenty-five.

The GR 91mm Model 1915 Russian trench mortar. The base made for ease of transport and reduced the likelihood of it sinking into the ground when fired. The sight was attached to the left of the frame and its maximum range was 500m. The Model 1916 differed in having a wheeled base.

Factory fresh, this captured German 90mm Lanz Model 1914 provided the inspiration for the Russian GR 91. The Austrians imported some 400 of this type but lost many during the Brusilov Offensive.

Possibly the strangest armoured vehicle ever designed came from the mind of Nicolai Lebedenko. He was given approval and funding to pursue his vision having demonstrated a clockwork model version to the Tsar in January 1915. Known as the 'Tsar tank' and powered by two engines from a downed Zeppelin, the prototype never made it further than the test ground. It was 9m high and would have been armed with up to fifteen machine guns and two 76mm cannon. It was abandoned in 1917 and scrapped several years later.

An officer makes observations from a ladder and a private fills cartridges in the foreground in a quiet sector of the front line. The wrapping around another private's rifle protects the mechanism from dirt and mud. The edges of the entrenching tool are sharpened for hand to hand combat.

A Maxim machine gun set up in an anti-aircraft role inside a fortification in the Pripet Marshes. As a result of the almost permanently waterlogged conditions, the defences across this 50–75km stretch of the front were based on islands that covered any possible approaches. The German positions were similar. Interestingly, both sides deployed large numbers of Polish troops in this area.

Hidden in a forest fastness, a Russian field hospital, partially underground, blends into its surroundings. Almost impassable and often trackless, the forests of western Russia provided a difficult battleground.

A regimental priest lectures his attentive flock on the merits of the trench club he is brandishing. Such extemporised weapons were produced in their millions by soldiers who required something less cumbersome than a rifle and bayonet when engaged in hand-to-hand combat in the narrow confines of a trench system.

In the shadow of the Kremlin a volunteer unit prepares to leave for the front prior to the Kerensky Offensive. The flag reads, 'the Union of Refugees and those returned from German captivity'. The Tsarist regime treated escaped POWs as potential subversives who were speeded off to obscure garrisons or the Caucasian Front. The Provisional government was more tolerant.

An artillery observation post in the front line corrects fire by telephone. Much of the telephone and electrical equipment was imported from Ericsson of Sweden.

Life in the line was not always blood and mud. An artistic soldier considers the woman of his dreams as sculpted in earth outside his dugout.

Chapter Eight

A Time to Hope, March–August 1917

While the Tsar consoled his wife, and many politicians, much of the upper classes and Stavka celebrated the demise of Rasputin. The bureaucrats prepared to host an inter-Allied conference in Petrograd which both Gurko and the new War Minister, General M.A. Beliaev, were scheduled to attend. The conference opened on 29 January 1917. With much discussion left to the civilians, the French and British military advisers, generals Castelnau and Wilson, left to tour the front. Wilson reported positively on N Front's condition, while the Frenchman was not impressed by anything, in short he did not think they were 'in a position to hold the *Boche* [German] divisions in front of them'. However, it was the Western civilians who heard the political gossip that was highly unfavourable to the dynasty. Indeed, the French ambassador summed up the situation in a telling sentence, 'Russia is walking into the abyss.' What all concluded was that the Tsar would be replaced by a form of constitutional monarchy or a republic but would not, all parties had assured them, abandon the Allied cause. Having agreed to increase supplies of aircraft, aero engines, heavy artillery and other munitions, the delegates returned to their countries. Gurko left for Stavka pleased with having postponed the Russian offensive until May at the earliest as time was still needed to push through his reforms. Having bid farewell to the Allied representatives, the Tsar returned to Stavka on 7 March leaving behind a capital that was seething with unrest.

The anniversary of Bloody Sunday fell on 22 January, and this event had been one of the catalysts that caused the 1905 Revolution. In 1917 it generated a series of demonstrations and strikes that became increasingly militant and disruptive, particularly in Petrograd. Indeed, Cossacks who patrolled the streets in support of the police were noted by the secret police as being 'on the side of the workers'. Further unrest, charged by a lack of bread and fuel among other things, in early March became rapidly uncontrollable and then the troops of the Petrograd garrison switched sides. The Duma, in session from late February, refused to dissolve itself and, almost without bloodshed or before anyone really understood what was happening, the long-anticipated revolution had taken place. By mid-March a Provisional Government had established itself in Petrograd, promising to hand over power to an elected Constituent Assembly later in the year. Simultaneously, a more radical organisation, the Council of Workers and Soldiers' Deputies, was set up almost as a rival government; it was better known as the Petrograd Soviet. On 15 March the Tsar abdicated in favour of his brother, the Grand Duke Michael, his last imperial act being the reinstatement of the Grand Duke Nicholas as Supreme Commander-in-Chief. However, neither of these orders came to pass.

Nicholas Romanov, the former Tsar, travelled back to Petrograd and house arrest at his palace complex of Tsarskoe Selo, outside Petrograd. Within ten days of the abdication the USA and the Allied governments had recognised the Provisional Government, having received reassurances that it would continue fighting. What they had all apparently overlooked was the horrific effect that an order issued by the Petrograd Soviet would have not only on the Petrograd garrison, for which it was solely intended, but on Russia's entire military structure. Order Number One gave all military units the right to elect committees to represent themselves. These committees would take over control of all weapons and reserved the right to disobey orders that contradicted those of the Soviet. Other issues less important but equally corrosive of discipline completed this historic document. A committee that included the former War Minister Polivanov was established to draw up a Declaration of Soldiers' Rights, which would fundamentally change the military regulations and further diminish the power of the officer corps. The terms of Order Number One spread through the armed forces like wildfire and within days committees sprang up in every unit ranging in political hue from deepest red to palest pink.

In the absence of the Grand Duke Nicholas Alexeyev became Supreme Commander-in-Chief with General A.I. Denikin as his Chief-of-Staff. Gurko was named commander of W Front; General A.N. Dragomirov N Front; Brusilov remained at SW Front; and General D.G. Shcherbachev was in charge of the Romanian Front. However optimistic Alexeyev may have felt earlier that month, by 26 March he was admitting that the army would not be in any condition to undertake an offensive until late May at the earliest. In the meantime, the new civilian War Minister, A.I. Guchkov, retired or dismissed, with Alexeyev's agreement, over 100 generals from N and W Fronts alone. During April non-commissioned military personnel aged 43 or over were discharged from service. This provoked a groundswell of desertion as those over 40 felt that they too should be allowed to go home.

The Central Powers' reaction was cautiously optimistic and they decided to do nothing that would provoke a reaction or revive the Russian soldiers' will to fight.

The exception to this was a short, sharp operation to eliminate the Russian bridgeheads on the Stokhod River. With the beginning of Easter on 15 April a period of fraternisation began all along the front. This played into the Central Powers' hands as they stepped up their well-orchestrated propaganda campaign that was designed to bring about a separate peace.

This was supported by the repatriation of V.I. Ulyanov, better known as Lenin, who, so they hoped, would cause even more trouble for the Provisional Government which showed no sign of suing for peace. Despite Order Number One, the increasingly problematic political situation in Petrograd and the declining authority of its officers, Stavka was determined to press ahead with the summer offensive. It was equally determined that the seaborne attack on Constantinople should proceed. However, it was pronouncements regarding Constantinople, among other issues, that brought the replacement of Guchkov by A.F. Kerensky as War Minister in mid-May. A member of the Petrograd Soviet, Kerensky was possessed of impressive oratorical powers and a charismatic manner as well as being trusted by the Soviet to protect its interests during Provisional Government cabinet meetings. Over the course of the next few weeks Kerensky became the dominant personality in the cabinet as a result of his influence with the Soviet.

Reinforcements once again began to flow from the depots to the front. However, a large number of the drafts from Petrograd carried with them an aura of rebelliousness, ill-discipline and a significantly less subservient attitude to authority. Following Kerensky's appointment as War Minister, Alexeyev and his front commanders travelled to the capital to discuss the crisis that poor discipline was creating. The resultant meeting produced a government statement in which Kerensky declared he would do everything within his power to restore the army and that 'The principles of democratising the army, and the organisation and strengthening of its military capacity for both defensive and offensive operations, shall be the first priority of the Provisional Government.' Lenin's riposte to this was that 'the essence of the new programme was offensive, offensive, offensive'. However, neither Bolshevik representatives from the front line or Lenin himself were unable to convince the Bolshevik Central Committee to veto support for the offensive.

With the Bolsheviks marginalised, the members of the Provisional Government almost unanimously in support and the front commanders more confident that their men would fight, Alexeyev, on 3 June, ordered N, W, and SW Fronts to be ready to carry out a series of co-ordinated attacks during the first week of July. As outlined earlier, SW Front's Seventh and Eleventh armies would attack towards Lemberg supported by more than 750 guns of the TAON (XLVIII Army Corps). To prevent reserves moving to counter this, N Front's Fifth Army and W Front's Tenth Army would mount strong diversionary attacks towards Vilna.

Gurko wrote enthusiastically that on W Front, 'All new methods which had been worked out in the earlier years of the campaign were adopted. At first attention was paid to combined artillery and aviation . . .'. Then, on 4 June, Kerensky replaced Alexeyev with Brusilov, Gurko with Denikin, while General A.E. Gutor took over SW Front. Thankfully, there was no change in the plan. When the Russian gunners began their pre-offensive bombardment along the fronts of Seventh and Eleventh armies the infantry were amazed at the intensity. Never before had they witnessed such pyrotechnics from their own side. For two days the guns battered away at the enemy lines, then, in the early hours of Sunday 1 July, the Russian infantry went over the top.

A veteran of the 1st Shock Detachment (later the Kornilov Regiment) described the first moments: 'When it got dark they made final preparations for the attack. Teams with clippers cut the wire to create gaps. The exit points were from the machine gun nests . . . No-one could see the full battlefield, since it was covered in a gunpowder haze, but they all rushed out of their trenches and rushed towards the enemy's . . .'. Elsewhere a member of the RNACD resorted to throwing hesitant Russian troops over the parapet. Only informed of the successes of Seventh and Eleventh armies, Kerensky hastened from his front-line observation post to Petrograd. Overjoyed with the advances of the 'freest army in the world', Kerensky commanded that the attacking units be rewarded with special 'Red Banners of the Revolution' and the honorific title 'Regiments of 18 June' (old-style dating). Unfortunately, the optimism of the first day was to evaporate almost overnight. As the attacking formations pushed forwards up to 30km, supporting units simply refused to move up. As the offensive's impetus diminished, the Austro-Germans began to recover and to organise counterattacks. Exhausted and lacking reserves, the forward Russian troops began to give ground. By 2 July Seventh Army had almost stopped fighting to be swiftly followed by Eleventh Army. General L.G. Kornilov's Eighth Army was ordered to attack on 6 July to relieve the pressure elsewhere on SW Front. But once again initial success was followed by a defiant lack of support. The Central Powers' major counterattack was launched on 19 July and hit Eleventh Army like a bolt from the blue and it rapidly began to collapse putting the rear of Third Army in jeopardy. Eighth Army too was in peril and SW Front began to retire in places up to 130km but maintained contact with Romanian Front.

On 21 July Kornilov was promoted to command of SW Front and he immediately re-introduced firm measures to deal with unauthorised retreats. Two days later, supported by Brusilov, Kornilov demanded, and got, the re-introduction of the death penalty in front-line areas with the support of both the Petrograd Soviet and the Provisional Government.

Less than a week later Kornilov replaced Brusilov as Supreme Commander-in-Chief with effect from 1 August. Certainly, on SW Front stability was restored relatively quickly as round-ups of agitators were carried out with ruthless efficiency. However, this was not the case on W or N Fronts where such characters found safety in Minsk, Riga or Petrograd. But among the rank and file along the line the rumour spread that the collapse of the front had been somehow engineered by the staff to pressure the Provisional Government into a return to old-regime methods of discipline.

Having retired onto Russian territory, many of SW Front's units became calmer as they felt they were now defending their homeland and once again fought with something akin to enthusiasm. The efforts of N and W Fronts which attacked on 22 July were in essence a replication of SW Front's. Such advances as were made were due to the sacrifices of the new Shock or Death formations and these were thrown away within hours by the lack of support. Sensibly, Denikin cancelled Tenth Army's offensive on 24 July. With both fronts back to their start lines the so-called Kerensky Offensive had ground to an inglorious halt.

In the trenches and the rear areas mistrust of officers was growing and gradually the siren calls of the simple Bolshevik slogans of 'Peace, bread and land' took hold of the men's consciousness. A Stavka report ominously noted during the summer of 1917:

> In the more tranquil units the new measures served to create a healthy climate but in the less dependable units they only magnify the unrest since the soldiers regard the orders on discipline and the death penalty as a return to the old regime and blame officers for their publication. The situation of officers is very bad, even critical.

The picture that emerges from this and similar reports is one of the crust on a stream of lava, firm to the casual observer but on closer inspection brittle, barely concealing a torrent of rage, frustration and danger. It would only take a single incautious step to fracture this veneer of calm to unleash uncontrollable forces.

The Inter-Allied conference in Petrograd was an occasion of much debate regarding the future of Russia's monarchy. Tsar Nicholas II, seen here with his back to the camera talking to officers and civil servants, was increasingly being viewed as 'yesterday's man'. Nevertheless, he continued to wield enormous power.

The leader of the mutiny by the *Volynsky* Guards Regiment, Sergeant Timofei Kirpichnikov. The speed of the old regime's collapse took all concerned by surprise. For his bravery and qualities of leadership, the Petrograd Soviet demanded he be awarded the St George's Cross, seen here. The disloyalty of such trusted regiments contributed to the Tsar's decision to abdicate.

Marching across one of Petrograd's bridges, the Guard *Equipage* (Marines) carry pro-revolutionary banners behind their band. Commanded by the Tsar's cousin, such displays of anti-monarchist feeling made it clear that few if any were prepared to fight for the Romanovs. The unit was on its way to swear allegiance to the Provisional Government.

Men of the Teke Cavalry Regiment swear loyalty to the Provisional Government. Volunteers from the Moslem Tekin tribe of Turkestan, they wore a distinctive, tall fleece cap throughout the year. They would become the bodyguard unit for General L.G. Kornilov when he became Supreme Commander-in-Chief later that year. The oath-swearing ceremonies of March 1917 usually involved removing monarchist symbols from standards and their replacement with red insignia.

As well as fraternising with enemy troops the front-line troops hosted thousands of agitators, who spread word of events in the capital and elsewhere. These civilians ranged from factory workers to political representatives of the Bolshevik, Socialist Revolutionary and other parties of the centre and left. They were instrumental in organising the unit committees that sprang up following the abdication.

As their authority declined, many officers formed themselves into organisations such as the Union of Officers to protect their interests and careers. However, this was considered counter-revolutionary and viewed with deep resentment by the rank and file. Many officers were enthusiastic in their support of the revolution, and the atrocities allegedly committed against the officer corps were not as widespread as later reported.

A brand new 122mm howitzer belonging to 32nd Mortar *Divizion* (half-regiment) is moved into position. Munitions production began to drop in the wake of the March Revolution as workers agitated for more pay, reduced hours and better conditions. However, the lack of activity meant that stocks were more than adequate throughout 1917. The technical branches of the army were less susceptible to political agitation than the infantry.

Marching proudly through the streets of Petrograd beneath a banner declaring 'Long live the Russian Federative Republic and Autonomous Estonia', Estonian troops call for independence. Other nationalist groups from Poland, Ukraine and the populations of the Caucasus claimed their freedom. The Provisional Government hoped to delay such events until the war ended.

Lenin, leader of the Bolshevik Party, returned from exile in April 1917. His party's organisational capabilities, centralised control structure and ruthless propaganda campaign played havoc with the Provisional Government's efforts to keep Russia in the war. Lenin's clear simple goals, 'all power to the Soviet, peace bread and land', struck chords in the politically unsophisticated minds of the soldiery and led to increasing support for his party during 1917 as war weariness and frustration with the Provisional Government grew.

Shown here in Riga with a group of committee members, A.F. Kerensky, centre with hand in jacket, undertook a series of tours of the front line prior to the summer offensive in an attempt to bolster the troops' morale. The effect of these lectures were positive in the short term but lacked the long-term drip feed of propaganda disseminated by Bolshevik newssheets such as *Soldiers' Truth*.

A Ruston tractor tows what appears to be a Vickers 127mm, 60-pounder gun on a mark 2 carriage. Such weapons were gathered into the TAON, which was Russia's most mechanised unit. Other British imports included the Vickers 234mm howitzer which the TAON deployed in four two-gun batteries behind SW Front. Two batteries of Vickers 305mm howitzers, along with similar monsters, were lost as they proved too immobile to withdraw when the TAON had to retreat.

Support from the rear was not uncommon as groups of workers and others adopted units at the front, mimicking the old regime's honorific regimental titles. Here a delegation of workers from the 'Respirator' factory brings a flag for the 15th Siberian Regiment. The flag's slogan reads 'The fighters of the factory for the fighters of the front.' The regiment was part of II Siberian Army Corps in position near Riga.

The 1st Russian Women's Battalion of Death parades its flag decorated with the name of its commander, Lieutenant M. (Maria) L. Bochkareva, a veteran soldier of two years' service. The unit was posted to W Front, where it went over the top and suffered severe casualties. Several other female units were formed at this time.

Waiting for the order to attack to come was always a nerve-wracking time. Russian troops had traditionally been issued with new underwear prior to an offensive and the men here are inspecting such garments. Fur caps under the old regulations should not have been worn during the spring but the men here have clearly ignored such directives, opting for the warmer alternative.

Men of the RNACD train troopers of the Caucasian Native Cavalry Division (CNCD) to use machine guns. Both units, the British on very few occasions, were used to enforce Kornilov's disciplinary edicts during the retreat of SW Front. A unit of mainly Moslem volunteers, the CNCD, better known by its nickname of the 'Savage Division', was to be sent north as part of the Petrograd Army during August 1917.

The first in a remarkable sequence of images taken by members of the RNACD during the retreat of SW Front. This incident involved the RNACD's Russian liaison officer, Captain Baron Girard, on detachment from 10th Novgorod Dragoons. Disgusted at what he perceived as blatant cowardice, Girard berated the retreating Russians and demanded they form up and await orders. Locker-Lampson forbade any of the British officers to become involved other than to direct traffic off the road, as seen here.

Incredibly, the men obeyed the Baron, and some, as Locker-Lampson noted, 'fell on their knees making the sign of the cross and prayed for mercy'. Girard's colleague, Lieutenant Reppmann, in light tunic near the lorry, then demanded the regimental colours be displayed. Girard himself is seen walking to the right armed with a pistol and walking stick to organise the forming ranks.

Seen here with Lieutenant Reppmann, second from left, Locker-Lampson, in a raincoat, discusses the situation with another RNACD officer, armed with a Lewis gun. It is possible that the photographs were taken by the *Daily Mirror* correspondent Mr Mewes.

Having refused to leave for the front, the men of the 1st Machine Gun Regiment added their weight to the uprising of 15 July when a group of militant Bolsheviks and anarchists decided the time had come to overthrow the Provisional Government. The so-called July Days, which lasted for five days, ran beyond the control of Lenin and Trotsky, who did not fully support the uprising.

When troops from the front and other units loyal to the Provisional Government reached Petrograd, such as the men of the Fifth Armoured *Divizion* (half regiment) seen here fraternising with the Petrograd St George's Battalion, arrived the uprising was crushed. The vehicle is an Austin Mark I and the location is Palace Square. When Trotsky was arrested and Lenin went into hiding for some months their influence was marginalised.

Throughout the summer the officers watched and waited, many hoping for a revival of the old rules and regulations. Most of the men waited to see who would act in their best interests. The situation on the home and war fronts was now steadily building towards critical mass.

Images and reports in the right-wing press blamed the failure of the Kerensky Offensive squarely on the shoulders of the Bolshevised troops who opened the front to the enemy. This training picture was typical of images used to reinforce the message of the soldiers' cowardly and traitorous behaviour. Subsequent inquiries, conducted by Stavka, demonstrated how far from the truth such stories were. By then, however, the damage had been done and the rift between the *Frontoviki* (front-line men) and the Provisional Government grew ever wider as the authorities also appeared to blame the men.

Chapter Nine

A Time to Despair, August 1917–March 1918

Kornilov's appointment as Supreme Commander-in-Chief was rapidly followed by Kerensky's promotion to head of the Provisional Government's cabinet on 4 August. In an amazing display of tactlessness Kerensky installed himself in the Romanovs' Winter Palace in Petrograd, gaining the nickname of Alexander IV in the process. Now the scene was set for the collapse of the Provisional Government and its replacement by a more brutal coalition headed by Lenin's Bolsheviks.

As August drew on Kornilov pressed ahead with his twin schemes of restoring discipline and the establishment of an army specifically created to defend Petrograd from both internal and external enemies – the Petrograd Army under the leadership of General A.M. Krymov. Kornilov also proposed to extend military law into the rear areas where reserve and replacement units were based, including cities such as Moscow, Kiev, Minsk and Kharkov. As an extension of this militarisation of the rear, munitions factories and the railway network would be subject to martial law. Although Kerensky prevaricated, the Petrograd Soviet now declared itself against the death penalty and an extension of martial law in the rear thus sparking a bitter war of words in the press. The right wing was growing desperate for a strong leader, a role for which Kornilov seemed eminently suited, although the left and centre groups portrayed him in an increasingly reactionary light. The Provisional Government, therefore, decided to hold a state conference to restore national unity and, to avoid the supercharged atmosphere of Petrograd, it was scheduled to be held in Moscow in late August.

Kornilov arrived ostentatiously but his low-key speech included, in defiance of Kerensky's orders, a list of his requirements to restore the army to fighting order including the restoration of the death penalty.

Once more fate intervened in the form of the German General Staff. For several months they had been waiting for an opportune moment to make an attempt on the city of Riga. Although the defences were considered strong, the morale of Twelfth Army, responsible for the city's defence, was, by September 1917, judged to be low enough to risk an attack. Although infantry strength was roughly equal, the Germans had moved virtually all their heavy artillery, some 250 guns, from all along the Eastern Front to positions facing Riga where the Russian defences ran along the Duna River. The German plan was to attack upstream of the city where, although the river was 350–400m wide, there were good landing points.

Unsurprisingly, assembling the men and equipment for this operation did not go unnoticed and the Russians drew up a plan to evacuate the city should the need arise.

Commencing at 0400hr on 1 September, the German bombardment lasted for 2 hours. A lethal cocktail of high-explosive and gas shells swept away the defenders so that from 0830hr the infantry, although highly vulnerable in the pontoons carrying them, tumbled ashore and within 2 hours had established a sizeable bridgehead. Unfortunately for the Germans, the speed of their crossing was so unexpected that the supporting troops could not cross quickly enough to exploit it. The Russians abandoned their bridgeheads on the western bank and the city itself was evacuated. By 3 September the line was re-established 32km to the north-east. Three days later Kerensky approved the formation of the Petrograd Army. By this time, however, Kornilov had issued a statement blaming 'hordes of Bolshevised mutineers' for the loss of Riga. It was this pronouncement that recalled in the minds of many the words he had used at the Moscow conference, 'it may take the fall of Riga to bring about the restoration of order in the rear'. As troops moved towards the Petrograd Army's assembly points, Kerensky and Kornilov squared up to one another and the confusing series of events that became known as the Kornilov Affair began. In brief, the influential forces of right and left coalesced behind their figureheads, Kornilov and Kerensky respectively. The left saw the Petrograd Army as the force that Kornilov would use to crush them, while the men of the Petrograd Army were told that they were going to suppress a counter revolution and defend the capital. Telephone calls, telexes and telegrams whizzed back and forth between all those concerned directly and indirectly heaping chaos on confusion hourly. Finally, on 10 September Kornilov announced, 'the Provisional Government under pressure from the Bolsheviks . . . is acting in full accord with the plans of the German General Staff . . .'. This pronouncement immediately cost him the support of two front commanders and many of his civilian backers. Within five days the Petrograd Army had been halted, Kornilov imprisoned for mutiny and General M.V. Alexeyev hauled out of retirement and restored to the post of Chief-of-Staff to Kerensky as Supreme Commander-in-Chief. Alexeyev resigned a week later, his replacement being General N.N. Dukhonin. Alexeyev's resignation letter cited three reasons for his departure, the Kornilov Affair, the state of the army (which he believed to be incapable of defending the Motherland) and his inability to help his brother officers, who he described as 'martyrs, dying without a murmur both from enemy bullets and from torture at the hands of their own troops'.

The mutual recrimination of Kerensky and Kornilov only served to further erode the men's confidence in all current authority and its representatives. Indeed, from mid-September, there was virtually no government as the cabinet had resigned en masse and power now lay almost exclusively with Kerensky, who declared Russia a republic on 14 September. On the same day the committee newssheet of Eighth Army accused Stavka of lying about the accounts of the fall of Tarnopol and Riga. This was a message that was to be repeated time and again along the length of the front and in the rear. One of the epithets flung at those who displayed any form of support for discipline beyond those defined by Kerensky or increasingly the Petrograd Soviet was 'Kornilovite'. It was a word that would be heard with increasing frequency during the next few months, gaining the status of a curse. More radical committee men were now calling for the death penalty for Kornilov and his adherents and it was a demand frequently taken up by the lower ranks. This hardening attitude is best summed up by a resolution passed by a unit of Ninth Army, 'It is time to forget the politics of forgiveness and loving kindness . . . The army must be cleared once and for all of those who dream of the old regime.' In the minds of the front-line soldiers Kerensky's name was becoming synonymous with that of the counter-revolutionary Kornilov, so the question was now who could be trusted? A report from the Special Army for 22 September described the mood of the men as 'dangerous' and noted that they complained of poor food and clothing and thought only of peace. Among the men of Romanian Front, generally less politicised than elsewhere, a rumour gained widespread currency that the war would be over by late October that year. SW Front reported, 'discipline is declining with every passing day', and Romanian Front commented that, 'Arriving replacements are not only depraved with Bolshevism but infected with outright hooligan elements.' Far from the mainstream of political activity in Anatolia, Caucasian Front reported that, 'Arriving replacements are solidly Bolshevik, badly trained and entirely undisciplined.' Nevertheless, there was still sufficient discipline and order to ensure that the majority of replacements did reach their destinations. Then again what was the point of deserting and risking the associated stigma if the war was reaching its end?

Meanwhile, at German HQ it had been concluded that one more operation must be mounted to persuade the Russians to sue for peace as the loss of Riga had clearly generated insufficient motivation. This was a fine line for the Central Powers to cross because of their concern that too great a victory would revive Russia's martial ardour.

Consequently, an amphibious attempt was to be made in the Baltic Sea with the objective of taking a small group of islands at the mouth of the Gulf of Riga, which formed an outpost of the Petrograd defence system. Operation Albion lasted from 12–21 October and was a complete success for both the German army and navy. On 22 October the Petrograd Soviet accused Kerensky of 'Being ready to surrender Petrograd to the Germans' and formed a Revolutionary Committee of Defence. With Ukraine, Finland and various regions in the Caucasus becoming increasingly vocal in their demand for self-determination and Stavka in disarray Kerensky now controlled little more than the staff at the Winter Palace. A firm believer in justice running its course, he had imprisoned Kornilov and several of his followers awaiting trial at the same time, releasing on bail the Bolsheviks imprisoned following the so-called 'July Days'. Among their number was L.D. Trotsky who was eager to launch a Bolshevik coup.

On 7 November the Bolsheviks struck. Petrograd fell into their hands that night and the next day the rump of the Provisional Government was arrested when the Winter Palace was occupied with almost no bloodshed. Kerensky had escaped to the HQ of N Front at Pskov, and from there he attempted to activate the remains of the Petrograd Army to regain control of the capital. Men of 1st Don Cossack Division along with a handful of infantry set out for Petrograd under the command of General P.N. Krasnov. However, once again, chaos and confusion disrupted both sides' lines of communication as both sought to rally support. This muddied the waters so much that most soldiers in the region chose neutrality fearing the onset of civil war. Therefore, the climax of the November Revolution focused on the Pulkovo Heights where Krasnov's 2,000 men faced up to 15,000 Red Guards stiffened with sailors from the Baltic Sea Fleet. After some desultory fighting, both sides began fraternising with the result that the Cossacks announced, 'Kerensky cooked up this mess, let him digest it' and promptly left for home. As his military support melted away, Kerensky fled into exile. It was 14 November and now the Bolsheviks had to muster support further afield.

By early December, as a result of a massive propaganda campaign, the Bolsheviks had gained control of the committees of N and W Fronts and made considerable headway elsewhere. From 7 November onwards Lenin's call for peace had garnered massive support from the armed forces.

This was followed up by his order to General Dukhonin at Stavka on 21 November to 'Contact the enemy military authorities with an offer of the immediate cessation of hostilities for the purpose of opening up peace negotiations.' A junior officer, N.V. Krylenko, had been appointed Commissar for War and he had already sent a team of negotiators across the lines to speak to the Germans, who had responded with an offer to open discussions at Brest Litovsk on 2 December. Upon reaching Stavka, Krylenko found that Dukhonin had done nothing and stood aside while Dukhonin was brutally murdered. A new 'revolutionary' Stavka was then established dedicated to ending the war.

On 15 December 1917 Russian representatives signed a general armistice with the Central Powers that was to last until 14 January 1918. Peace talks proper began on 8 January but now included a separate Ukrainian delegation. Russia's senior negotiator, Trotsky, dragged out the talks hoping for revolution in Germany and Austria but was undermined when the Ukrainians signed a treaty on 9 February. The following day Trotsky declared, 'We are going out of the war, but . . . refuse to sign the peace treaty . . . Russian troops are receiving an order for general demobilisation on all lines of the fronts.'

On 18 February, frustrated by Bolshevik delaying tactics, the Austro-Germans began to advance into Russia as well as landing troops in newly independent Finland, a short march from Petrograd. Lenin, in the teeth of fierce opposition from other parties and many of his own Bolsheviks, pushed through a measure accepting the brutally harsh peace now on offer. On 3 March the Russian delegation signed the Treaty of Brest Litovsk, officially ending Russia's participation in the First World War. What had begun in the gilded palaces of the Romanov dynasty was ended in an array of temporary buildings in the grounds of a burned out Tsarist fortress. Meanwhile, to the south, around Rostov on Don, generals Kornilov and Alexeyev had gathered what was to be the Bolshevik's next major enemy, the Volunteer Army. The revolutionaries of November had ended one war only to enter into another, the Russian Civil War.

Technical units such as this armoured car
Divizion tended to retain their discipline
throughout the upheavals of 1917. This group
includes a Garford lorry mounting a modified
76mm mountain gun in a rear facing turret.

One of the formations destined for the
Petrograd Army was the Caucasian
Native Cavalry Division. These Moslem
volunteers were persuaded by Soviet
representatives that they were being
used to crush the Provisional
Government, an argument that they
found sufficiently convincing to
withdraw their support for Kornilov.
The flag seen here is that of the Tartar
Regiment.

A Russian front-line position, 1917. The men are sporting metal gas-mask containers, as was common by this time. The filters were effective for up to 2 hours but the men's ability to function diminished rapidly during that time. Although the Russian gunners at Riga (and along the Stokhod River) had been issued the Avalov mask, one of the best available, the Germans noted little gunnery during the Riga attack after 0700hr.

In some parts of the line the men continued to carry out their duties as long as they were defensive in nature. This wiring party is typical of such work.

A German officer poses inside a Russian artillery bunker, a part of the Riga defences. Although a gas mask was available for horses under bombardment, it would have been a brave man who tried to fit one. Many of the 200 guns that were lost were either abandoned for this reason or were fixed position, immobile coastal defence pieces.

Sailors of the Baltic Sea Fleet, such as this man, provided a solid foundation for the Bolsheviks' armed support. A group of such soldiers were the mainstay of the forces deployed to protect Petrograd against Krasnov's Cossacks.

Some of the Bolshevik supporters captured on film following the Battle of Pulkovo Heights.

During 1917 Britain attempted to dispel the Russians' perception that her armed forces were not pulling their weight. On the extreme right of the front row is Colonel A.C. Bromhead, head of British Gaumont, who led a propaganda mission that showed footage of the Western Front to Russian troops and civilians. It was too little too late.

Despite fighting well throughout the summer, the Romanian army was still heavily dependent on the Russians. When overtures regarding peace began the Romanians found themselves increasingly isolated as the Russians negotiated. The blindfolded Austrian soldiers seen here have crossed the lines in Romania to discuss terms.

The first Russian delegation arrives at Brest Litovsk, led by A.A. Joffe (doffing bowler hat) with L.B. Kamenev (Trotsky's brother-in-law, on the extreme right). Both were influential members of the Petrograd Soviet. Neither claimed proletarian roots, indeed Joffe's father was a millionaire.

Joffe, Kamenev and Rear Admiral V.M. Altvater (right) stroll back to their quarters at Brest Litovsk. Altvater had been instrumental in the politicising of the Baltic Sea Fleet before and during the March Revolution. Politically reliable, he was the naval representative during the negotiations.

As the first Russian military delegate, Major General V.E. Skalon, had committed suicide within hours of his arrival, Major General A.A. Samoilov was dispatched as his replacement. Samoilov (right centre) is seen speaking to a German officer following his arrival.

The building in which the negotiations were carried out was less than imposing but comfortable given the season.

In the office of the Russian delegation was this Hughes apparatus, an early form of teleprinter. The civilian is the delegation's secretary, L.M. Karahan, who was a member of the Petrograd Soviet. The telegraphist and the officer were detached from Stavka for technical support.

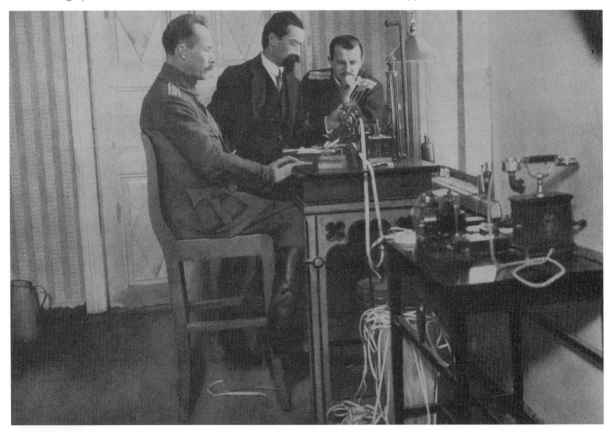

The Ukrainian delegation socialises with officers from Germany and Austria. Less than four months after the Ukrainians signed the treaty Kiev was occupied by the Germans and effectively a fiefdom of the Central Powers. This image was taken outside the White Palace where the treaties with both Ukraine and Russia were signed.

The second Russian delegation was led by Trotsky, seen here facing the camera and leaving for Petrograd having declared 'no peace, no war'. To his rear is Joffe, with his back to the camera, Altvater and Kamenev.

The pickets that held the front line as the Russian armies demobilised in the early weeks of 1918 often consisted of groups of men such as these. Naturally, such tiny groups were no match for the forces of the Central Powers when they unleashed Operation Thunderbolt in February 1918.

The popular image of Russian troops bolting for the trains did not apply to every unit following the demobilisation order. For many troops the camaraderie of the front had been immensely important. Officers and men often wept as their regiment dispersed for the last time.